EVERYMAN,
I WILL GO WITH THEE
AND BE THY GUIDE,
IN THY MOST NEED
TO GO BY THY SIDE

Robert and Elizabeth Barrett Browning

Poems and Letters

EVERYMAN'S LIBRARY

POCKET POETS

Alfred A. Knopf · New York · Toronto

THIS IS A BORZOI BOOK
PUBLISHED BY ALFRED A. KNOPF

This selection by Peter Washington first published in
Everyman's Library, 2003
Copyright © 2003 by Everyman's Library

www.randomhouse.com/everymans

ISBN 1-4000-4022-1

Typography by Peter B. Willberg
Typeset in the UK by AccComputing, North Barrow, Somerset
Printed and bound in Germany by GGP Media, Pössneck

CONTENTS

ELIZABETH BARRETT BROWNING

FOREWORD

More than a century after Robert Browning's death, he and Elizabeth Barrett are still English poetry's most celebrated married couple. This collection of poems and letters takes their relationship as its main theme, emphasizing the intimate, lyrical aspects of their work at the expense of poems which are more familiar. Both were superb story-tellers, especially Robert who equals the great nineteenth-century novelists in his ability to create characters. Elizabeth, too, was at her best in the little-known verse-novel *Aurora Leigh*, which is a finer work than the more celebrated *Sonnets from the Portuguese*. Examples of their narrative skills are included in this volume, but pride of place is given to shorter poems and extracts from letters in order to throw light on two intriguing characters and their complex involvement.

Few of the poems selected are directly autobiographical in the contemporary sense – Robert and Elizabeth are most certainly *not* Sylvia and Ted – but that hardly matters, such is the strength, directness and vividness of their voices. Like other Victorian writers, they were large characters with wide interests, many of which are represented here, not least their love of Italy and their intense dialogue about the nature of poetry. But, above all, it is as individuals that I have tried to show them: as friends, lovers, colleagues, husband and wife.

PETER WASHINGTON

ROBERT BROWNING

LOVE

So, the year's done with!
  (*Love me for ever!*)
All March begun with,
  April's endeavour;
May-wreaths that bound me
  June needs must sever;
Now snows fall round me,
  Quenching June's fever –
  (*Love me for ever!*)

LOVE IN A LIFE

Room after room,
I hunt the house through
We inhabit together.
Heart, fear nothing, for, heart, thou shalt find her –
Next time, herself! – not the trouble behind her
Left in the curtain, the couch's perfume!
As she brushed it, the cornice-wreath blossomed anew:
Yon looking-glass gleamed at the wave of her feather.

Yet the day wears,
And door succeeds door;
I try the fresh fortune –
Range the wide house from the wing to the centre.
Still the same chance! she goes out as I enter.
Spend my whole day in the quest, – who cares?
But 'tis twilight, you see, – with such suites to explore,
Such closets to search, such alcoves to importune!

LIFE IN A LOVE

Escape me?
Never –
Beloved!
While I am I, and you are you,
   So long as the world contains us both,
   Me the loving and you the loth,
While the one eludes, must the other pursue.
My life is a fault at last, I fear:
   It seems too much like a fate, indeed!
   Though I do my best I shall scarce succeed.
But what if I fail of my purpose here?
It is but to keep the nerves at strain,
   To dry one's eyes and laugh at a fall,
And, baffled, get up and begin again, –
   So the chase takes up one's life, that's all.
While, look but once from your farthest bound
   At me so deep in the dust and dark,
No sooner the old hope goes to ground
   Than a new one, straight to the self-same mark,
I shape me –
Ever
Removed!

ONE WAY OF LOVE

All June I bound the rose in sheaves.
Now, rose by rose, I strip the leaves
And strew them where Pauline may pass.
She will not turn aside? Alas!
Let them lie. Suppose they die?
The chance was they might take her eye.

How many a month I strove to suit
These stubborn fingers to the lute!
To-day I venture all I know.
She will not hear my music? So!
Break the string; fold music's wing:
Suppose Pauline had bade me sing!

My whole life long I learned to love.
This hour my utmost art I prove
And speak my passion – heaven or hell?
She will not give me heaven? 'Tis well!
Lose who may – I still can say,
Those who win heaven, blest are they!

ANOTHER WAY OF LOVE

June was not over
Though past the full,
And the best of her roses
Had yet to blow,
When a man I know
(But shall not discover,
Since ears are dull,
And time discloses)
Turned him and said with a man's true air,
Half sighing a smile in a yawn, as 'twere, –
'If I tire of your June, will she greatly care?'

Well, dear, in-doors with you!
True! serene deadness
Tries a man's temper.
What's in the blossom
June wears on her bosom?
Can it clear scores with you?
Sweetness and redness.
Eadem semper!
Go, let me care for it greatly or slightly!
If June mend her bower now, your hand left unsightly
By plucking the roses, – my June will do rightly.

And after, for pastime,
    If June be refulgent
With flowers in completeness,
    All petals, no prickles,
    Delicious as trickles
Of wine poured at mass-time, –
    And choose One indulgent
    To redness and sweetness:
Or if, with experience of man and of spider,
June use my June-lightning, the strong insect-ridder,
And stop the fresh film-work, – why, June will consider.

CRISTINA

She should never have looked at me
　　If she meant I should not love her!
There are plenty ... men, you call such,
　　I suppose ... she may discover
All her soul to, if she pleases,
　　And yet leave much as she found them:
But I'm not so, and she knew it
　　When she fixed me, glancing round them.

What? To fix me thus meant nothing?
　　But I can't tell (there's my weakness)
What her look said! – no vile cant, sure,
　　About 'need to strew the bleakness
'Of some lone shore with its pearl-seed.
　　'That the sea feels' – no 'strange yearning
'That such souls have, most to lavish
　　'Where there's chance of least returning.'

Oh, we're sunk enough here, God knows!
　　But not quite so sunk that moments,
Sure tho' seldom, are denied us,
　　When the spirit's true endowments
Stand out plainly from its false ones,
　　And apprise it if pursuing
Or the right way or the wrong way,
　　To its triumph or undoing.

There are flashes struck from midnights,
    There are fire-flames noondays kindle,
Whereby piled-up honours perish,
    Whereby swollen ambitions dwindle,
While just this or that poor impulse,
    Which for once had play unstifled,
Seems the sole work of a life-time
    That away the rest have trifled.

Doubt you if, in some such moment,
    As she fixed me, she felt clearly,
Ages past the soul existed,
    Here an age 'tis resting merely,
And hence fleets again for ages,
    While the true end, sole and single,
It stops here for is, this love-way,
    With some other soul to mingle?

Else it loses what it lived for,
    And eternally must lose it;
Better ends may be in prospect,
    Deeper blisses (if you choose it),
But this life's end and this love-bliss
    Have been lost here. Doubt you whether
This she felt as, looking at me,
    Mine and her souls rushed together?

Oh, observe! Of course, next moment,
　　The world's honours, in derision,
Trampled out the light for ever:
　　Never fear but there's provision
Of the devil's to quench knowledge
　　Lest we walk the earth in rapture!
– Making those who catch God's secret
　　Just so much more prize their capture!

Such am I: the secret's mine now!
　　She has lost me, I have gained her;
Her soul's mine: and thus, grown perfect,
　　I shall pass my life's remainder.
Life will just hold out the proving
　　Both our powers, alone and blended:
And then, come next life quickly!
　　This world's use will have been ended.

PORPHYRIA'S LOVER

The rain set early in to-night,
    The sullen wind was soon awake,
It tore the elm-tops down for spite,
    And did its worst to vex the lake:
    I listened with heart fit to break.
When glided in Porphyria; straight
    She shut the cold out and the storm,
And kneeled and made the cheerless grate
    Blaze up, and all the cottage warm;
    Which done, she rose, and from her form
Withdrew the dripping cloak and shawl,
    And laid her soiled gloves by, untied
Her hat and let the damp hair fall,
    And, last, she sat down by my side
    And called me. When no voice replied,
She put my arm about her waist,
    And made her smooth white shoulder bare,
And all her yellow hair displaced,
    And, stooping, made my cheek lie there,
    And spread, o'er all, her yellow hair,
Murmuring how she loved me – she
    Too weak, for all her heart's endeavour,
To set its struggling passion free
    From pride, and vainer ties dissever,
    And give herself to me for ever.

But passion sometimes would prevail,
    Nor could to-night's gay feast restrain
A sudden thought of one so pale
    For love of her, and all in vain:
    So, she was come through wind and rain.
Be sure I looked up at her eyes
    Happy and proud; at last I knew
Porphyria worshipped me; surprise
    Made my heart swell, and still it grew
    While I debated what to do.
That moment she was mine, mine, fair,
    Perfectly pure and good: I found
A thing to do, and all her hair
    In one long yellow string I wound
    Three times her little throat around,
And strangled her. No pain felt she;
    I am quite sure she felt no pain.
As a shut bud that holds a bee,
    I warily oped her lids: again
    Laughed the blue eyes without a stain.
And I untightened next the tress
    About her neck; her cheek once more
Blushed bright beneath my burning kiss:
    I propped her head up as before,
    Only, this time my shoulder bore

Her head, which droops upon it still:
    The smiling rosy little head,
So glad it has its utmost will,
    That all it scorned at once is fled,
    And I, its love, am gained instead!
Porphyria's love: she guessed not how
    Her darling one wish would be heard.
And thus we sit together now,
    And all night long we have not stirred,
    And yet God has not said a word!

From PAULINE

Night, and one single ridge of narrow path
Between the sullen river and the woods
Waving and muttering, for the moonless night
Has shaped them into images of life,
Like the uprising of the giant-ghosts,
Looking on earth to know how their sons fare:
Thou art so close by me, the roughest swell
Of wind in the tree-tops hides not the panting
Of thy soft breasts. No, we will pass to morning –
Morning, the rocks and valleys and old woods.
How the sun brightens in the mist, and here,
Half in the air, like creatures of the place,
Trusting the element, living on high boughs
That swing in the wind – look at the silver spray
Flung from the foam-sheet of the cataract
Amid the broken rocks! Shall we stay here
With the wild hawks? No, ere the hot noon come,
Dive we down – safe! See this our new retreat
Walled in with a sloped mound of matted shrubs,
Dark, tangled, old and green, still sloping down
To a small pool whose waters lie asleep
Amid the trailing boughs turned water-plants:
And tall trees overarch to keep us in,
Breaking the sunbeams into emerald shafts,
And in the dreamy water one small group

Of two or three strange trees are got together
Wondering at all around, as strange beasts herd
Together far from their own land: all wildness,
No turf nor moss, for boughs and plants pave all,
And tongues of bank go shelving in the lymph,
Where the pale-throated snake reclines his head,
And old grey stones lie making eddies there,
The wild-mice cross them dry-shod. Deeper in!
Shut thy soft eyes – now look – still deeper in!
This is the very heart of the woods all round
Mountain-like heaped above us; yet even here
One pond of water gleams; far off the river
Sweeps like a sea, barred out from land; but one –
One thin clear sheet has overleaped and wound
Into this silent depth, which gained, it lies
Still, as but let by sufferance; the trees bend
O'er it as wild men watch a sleeping girl,
And through their roots long creeping plants
        out-stretch
Their twined hair, steeped and sparkling; farther on,
Tall rushes and thick flag-knots have combined
To narrow it; so, at length, a silver thread,
It winds, all noiselessly through the deep wood
Till thro' a cleft-way, thro' the moss and stone,
It joins its parent-river with a shout.

Up for the glowing day, leave the old woods!
See, they part like a ruined arch: the sky!
Nothing but sky appears, so close the roots
And grass of the hill-top level with the air –
Blue sunny air, where a great cloud floats laden
With light, like a dead whale that white birds pick,
Floating away in the sun in some north sea.
Air, air, fresh life-blood, thin and searching air,
The clear, dear breath of God that loveth us,
Where small birds reel and winds take their delight!
Water is beautiful, but not like air:
See, where the solid azure waters lie
Made as of thickened air, and down below,
The fern-ranks like a forest spread themselves
As though each pore could feel the element;
Where the quick glancing serpent winds his way,
Float with me there, Pauline! – but not like air.

THE LOST MISTRESS

All's over, then: does truth sound bitter
    As one at first believes?
Hark, 'tis the sparrows' good-night twitter
    About your cottage eaves!

And the leaf-buds on the vine are woolly,
    I noticed that, to-day;
One day more bursts them open fully
    – You know the red turns grey.

To-morrow we meet the same then, dearest?
    May I take your hand in mine?
Mere friends are we, – well, friends the merest
    Keep much that I resign:

For each glance of the eye so bright and black,
    Though I keep with heart's endeavour, –
Your voice, when you wish the snowdrops back,
    Though it stay in my soul for ever! –

Yet I will but say what mere friends say,
    Or only a thought stronger;
I will hold your hand but as long as all may,
    Or so very little longer!

MY LAST DUCHESS

FERRARA

That's my last Duchess painted on the wall,
Looking as if she were alive. I call
That piece a wonder, now: Frà Pandolf's hands
Worked busily a day, and there she stands.
Will't please you sit and look at her? I said
'Frà Pandolf' by design, for never read
Strangers like you that pictured countenance,
The depth and passion of its earnest glance,
But to myself they turned (since none puts by
The curtain I have drawn for you, but I)
And seemed as they would ask me, if they durst,
How such a glance came there; so, not the first
Are you to turn and ask thus. Sir, 'twas not
Her husband's presence only, called that spot
Of joy into the Duchess' cheek: perhaps
Frà Pandolf chanced to say 'Her mantle laps
'Over my lady's wrist too much,' or 'Paint
'Must never hope to reproduce the faint
'Half-flush that dies along her throat:' such stuff
Was courtesy, she thought, and cause enough
For calling up that spot of joy. She had
A heart – how shall I say? – too soon made glad,
Too easily impressed; she liked whate'er

She looked on, and her looks went everywhere.
Sir, 'twas all one! My favour at her breast,
The dropping of the daylight in the West,
The bough of cherries some officious fool
Broke in the orchard for her, the white mule
She rode with round the terrace – all and each
Would draw from her alike the approving speech,
Or blush, at least. She thanked men, – good!
      but thanked
Somehow – I know not how – as if she ranked
My gift of a nine-hundred-years-old name
With anybody's gift. Who'd stoop to blame
This sort of trifling? Even had you skill
In speech – (which I have not) – to make your will
Quite clear to such an one, and say, 'Just this
'Or that in you disgusts me; here you miss,
'Or there exceed the mark' – and if she let
Herself be lessoned so, nor plainly set
Her wits to yours, forsooth, and made excuse,
– E'en then would be some stooping; and I choose
Never to stoop. Oh sir, she smiled, no doubt,
Whene'er I passed her; but who passed without
Much the same smile? This grew; I gave commands;
Then all smiles stopped together. There she stands
As if alive. Will't please you rise? We'll meet
The company below, then. I repeat,
The Count your master's known munificence

Is ample warrant that no just pretence
Of mine for dowry will be disallowed;
Though his fair daughter's self, as I avowed
At starting, is my object. Nay, we'll go
Together down, sir. Notice Neptune, though,
Taming a sea-horse, thought a rarity,
Which Claus of Innsbruck cast in bronze for me!

EVELYN HOPE

Beautiful Evelyn Hope is dead!
    Sit and watch by her side an hour.
That is her book-shelf, this her bed;
    She plucked that piece of geranium-flower,
Beginning to die too, in the glass;
    Little has yet been changed, I think:
The shutters are shut, no light may pass
    Save two long rays thro' the hinge's chink.

Sixteen years old when she died!
    Perhaps she had scarcely heard my name;
It was not her time to love; beside,
    Her life had many a hope and aim,
Duties enough and little cares,
    And now was quiet, now astir,
Till God's hand beckoned unawares, –
    And the sweet white brow is all of her.

Is it too late then, Evelyn Hope?
    What, your soul was pure and true,
The good stars met in your horoscope,
    Made you of spirit, fire and dew –
And, just because I was thrice as old
    And our paths in the world diverged so wide,
Each was nought to each, must I be told?
    We were fellow mortals, nought beside?

No, indeed! for God above
    Is great to grant, as mighty to make,
And creates the love to reward the love:
    I claim you still, for my own love's sake!
Delayed it may be for more lives yet,
    Through worlds I shall traverse, not a few:
Much is to learn, much to forget
    Ere the time be come for taking you.

But the time will come, – at last it will,
    When, Evelyn Hope, what meant (I shall say)
In the lower earth, in the years long still,
    That body and soul so pure and gay?
Why your hair was amber, I shall divine,
    And your mouth of your own geranium's red –
And what you would do with me, in fine,
    In the new life come in the old one's stead.

I have lived (I shall say) so much since then,
    Given up myself so many times,
Gained me the gains of various men,
    Ransacked the ages, spoiled the climes;
Yet one thing, one, in my soul's full scope,
    Either I missed or itself missed me:
And I want and find you, Evelyn Hope!
    What is the issue? let us see!

I loved you, Evelyn, all the while.
　　My heart seemed full as it could hold?
There was place and to spare for the frank young smile,
　　And the red young mouth, and the hair's young gold.
So, hush, – I will give you this leaf to keep:
　　See, I shut it inside the sweet cold hand!
There, that is our secret: go to sleep!
　　You will wake, and remember, and understand.

NEVER THE TIME AND THE PLACE

Never the time and the place
    And the loved one all together!
This path – how soft to pace!
    This May – what magic weather!
    Where is the loved one's face?
In a dream that loved one's face meets mine,
    But the house is narrow, the place is bleak
Where, outside, rain and wind combine
    With a furtive ear, if I strive to speak,
    With a hostile eye at my flushing cheek,
With a malice that marks each word, each sign!
O enemy sly and serpentine,
    Uncoil thee from the waking man!
        Do I hold the Past
        Thus firm and fast
    Yet doubt if the Future hold I can?
This path so soft to pace shall lead
Thro' the magic of May to herself indeed!
Or narrow if needs the house must be,
Outside are the storms and strangers: we –
Oh, close, safe, warm sleep I and she,
– I and she!

NOW

Out of your whole life give but a moment!
All of your life that has gone before,
All to come after it, – so you ignore,
So you make perfect the present, – condense,
In a rapture of rage, for perfection's endowment,
Thought and feeling and soul and sense –
Merged in a moment which gives me at last
You around me for once, you beneath me, above me –
Me – sure that despite of time future, time past, –
This tick of our life-time's one moment you love me!
How long such suspension may linger? Ah, Sweet –
The moment eternal – just that and no more –
When ecstasy's utmost we clutch at the core
While cheeks burn, arms open, eyes shut and lips meet!

MEETING AT NIGHT

The grey sea and the long black land;
And the yellow half-moon large and low;
And the startled little waves that leap
In fiery ringlets from their sleep,
As I gain the cove with pushing prow,
And quench its speed i' the slushy sand.

Then a mile of warm sea-scented beach;
Three fields to cross till a farm appears;
A tap at the pane, the quick sharp scratch
And blue spurt of a lighted match,
And a voice less loud, thro' its joys and fears,
Than the two hearts beating each to each!

PARTING AT MORNING

Round the cape of a sudden came the sea,
And the sun looked over the mountain's rim:
And straight was a path of gold for him,
And the need of a world of men for me.

UP AT A VILLA – DOWN IN THE CITY
(AS DISTINGUISHED BY AN ITALIAN PERSON OF QUALITY)

Had I but plenty of money, money enough and to spare,
The house for me, no doubt, were a house in the
      city-square;
Ah, such a life, such a life, as one leads at the window
      there!

Something to see, by Bacchus, something to hear,
      at least!
There, the whole day long, one's life is a perfect feast;
While up at a villa one lives, I maintain it, no more
      than a beast.

Well now, look at our villa! stuck like the horn of
      a bull
Just on a mountain-edge as bare as the creature's skull,
Save a mere shag of a bush with hardly a leaf to pull!
– I scratch my own, sometimes, to see if the hair's
      turned wool.

But the city, oh the city – the square with the houses!
      Why?
They are stone-faced, white as a curd, there's
      something to take the eye!
Houses in four straight lines, not a single front awry;

You watch who crosses and gossips, who saunters,
     who hurries by;
Green blinds, as a matter of course, to draw when the
     sun gets high;
And the shops with fanciful signs which are painted
     properly.

What of a villa? Though winter be over in March
     by rights,
'Tis May perhaps ere the snow shall have withered
     well off the heights:
You've the brown ploughed land before, where the
     oxen steam and wheeze,
And the hills over-smoked behind by the faint grey
     olive-trees.

Is it better in May, I ask you? You've summer all at
     once;
In a day he leaps complete with a few strong April
     suns.
'Mid the sharp short emerald wheat, scarce risen three
     fingers well,
The wild tulip, at end of its tube, blows out its great
     red bell

Like a thin clear bubble of blood, for the children to
     pick and sell.

Is it ever hot in the square? There's a fountain to spout
     and splash!
In the shade it sings and springs; in the shine such
     foam-bows flash
On the horses with curling fish-tails, that prance and
     paddle and pash
Round the lady atop in her conch – fifty gazers do not
     abash,
Though all that she wears is some weeds round her
     waist in a sort of sash.

All the year long at the villa, nothing to see though you
     linger,
Except yon cypress that points like death's lean lifted
     forefinger.
Some think fireflies pretty, when they mix i' the corn
     and mingle,
Or thrid the stinking hemp till the stalks of it seem
     a-tingle.
Late August or early September, the stunning cicala
     is shrill,
And the bees keep their tiresome whine round the
     resinous firs on the hill.
Enough of the seasons, – I spare you the months of the
     fever and chill.

Ere you open your eyes in the city, the blessed church-
    bells begin:
No sooner the bells leave off than the diligence rattles in:
You get the pick of the news, and it costs you never
    a pin.
By-and-by there's the travelling doctor gives pills,
    lets blood, draws teeth;
Or the Pulcinello-trumpet breaks up the market
    beneath.
At the post-office such a scene-picture – the new play,
    piping hot!
And a notice how, only this morning, three liberal
    thieves were shot.
Above it, behold the Archbishop's most fatherly of
    rebukes,
And beneath, with his crown and his lion, some little
    new law of the Duke's!
Or a sonnet with flowery marge, to the Reverend Don
    So-and-so
Who is Dante, Boccaccio, Petrarca, Saint Jerome and
    Cicero,
'And moreover,' (the sonnet goes rhyming,) 'the skirts
    of Saint Paul has reached,
'Having preached us those six Lent-lectures more
    unctuous than ever he preached.'
Noon strikes, – here sweeps the procession! our Lady
    borne smiling and smart

With a pink gauze gown all spangles, and seven
    swords stuck in her heart!
Bang-whang-whang goes the drum, *tootle-te-tootle*
    the fife;
No keeping one's haunches still: it's the greatest
    pleasure in life.

But bless you, it's dear – it's dear! fowls, wine, at double
    the rate.
They have clapped a new tax upon salt, and what oil
    pays passing the gate
It's a horror to think of. And so, the villa for me, not
    the city!
Beggars can scarcely be choosers: but still – ah, the
    pity, the pity!
Look, two and two go the priests, then the monks with
    cowls and sandals,
And the penitents dressed in white shirts, a-holding
    the yellow candles;
One, he carries a flag up straight, and another a cross
    with handles,
And the Duke's guard brings up the rear, for the better
    prevention of scandals:
Bang-whang-whang goes the drum, *tootle-te-tootle*
    the fife.
Oh, a day in the city-square, there is no such pleasure
    in life!

A SERENADE AT THE VILLA

That was I, you heard last night,
    When there rose no moon at all,
Nor, to pierce the strained and tight
    Tent of heaven, a planet small:
Life was dead and so was light.

Not a twinkle from the fly,
    Not a glimmer from the worm;
When the crickets stopped their cry,
    When the owls forbore a term,
You heard music; that was I.

Earth turned in her sleep with pain,
    Sultrily suspired for proof:
In at heaven and out again,
    Lightning! – where it broke the roof,
Bloodlike, some few drops of rain.

What they could my words expressed,
    O my love, my all, my one!
Singing helped the verses best,
    And when singing's best was done,
To my lute I left the rest.

So wore night; the East was gray,
    White the broad-faced hemlock-flowers:
There would be another day;
    Ere its first of heavy hours
Found me, I had passed away.

What became of all the hopes,
    Words and song and lute as well?
Say, this struck you – 'When life gropes
    'Feebly for the path where fell
'Light last on the evening slopes,

'One friend in that path shall be,
    'To secure my step from wrong;
'One to count night day for me,
    'Patient through the watches long,
'Serving most with none to see.'

Never say – as something bodes –
    'So, the worst has yet a worse!
'When life halts 'neath double loads,
    'Better the taskmaster's curse
'Than such music on the roads!

'When no moon succeeds the sun,
    'Nor can pierce the midnight's tent
'Any star, the smallest one,
    'While some drops, where lightning rent,
'Show the final storm begun –

'When the fire-fly hides its spot,
    'When the garden-voices fail
'In the darkness thick and hot, –
    'Shall another voice avail,
'That shape be where these are not?

'Has some plague a longer lease,
    'Proffering its help uncouth?
'Can't one even die in peace?
    'As one shuts one's eyes on youth,
'Is that face the last one sees?'

Oh how dark your villa was,
    Windows fast and obdurate!
How the garden grudged me grass
    Where I stood – the iron gate
Ground its teeth to let me pass!

A TOCCATA OF GALUPPI'S

Oh Galuppi, Baldassaro, this is very sad to find!
I can hardly misconceive you; it would prove me deaf
   and blind;
But although I take your meaning, 'tis with such a
   heavy mind!

Here you come with your old music, and here's all the
   good it brings.
What, they lived once thus at Venice where the
   merchants were the kings,
Where Saint Mark's is, where the Doges used to wed
   the sea with rings?

Ay, because the sea's the street there; and 'tis arched by
   ... what you call
... Shylock's bridge with houses on it, where they kept
   the carnival:
I was never out of England – it's as if I saw it all.

Did young people take their pleasure when the sea was
   warm in May?
Balls and masks begun at midnight, burning ever to
   mid-day,
When they made up fresh adventures for the morrow,
   do you say?

Was a lady such a lady, cheeks so round and lips so red, –
On her neck the small face buoyant, like a bell-flower
    on its bed,
O'er the breast's superb abundance where a man might
    base his head?

Well, and it was graceful of them – they'd break talk off
    and afford
– She, to bite her mask's black velvet – he, to finger on
    his sword,
While you sat and played Toccatas, stately at the
    clavichord?

What? Those lesser thirds so plaintive, sixths
    diminished, sigh on sigh,
Told them something? Those suspensions, those
    solutions – 'Must we die?'
Those commiserating sevenths – 'Life might last!
    we can but try!'

'Were you happy?' – 'Yes.' – 'And are you still as
    happy?' – 'Yes. And you?'
– 'Then, more kisses!' – 'Did *I* stop them, when a
    million seemed so few?'
Hark, the dominant's persistence till it must be
    answered to!

So, an octave struck the answer. Oh, they praised you,
    I dare say!
'Brave Galuppi! that was music! good alike at grave
    and gay!
'I can always leave off talking when I hear a master
    play!'

Then they left you for their pleasure: till in due time,
    one by one,
Some with lives that came to nothing, some with deeds
    as well undone,
Death stepped tacitly and took them where they never
    see the sun.

But when I sit down to reason, think to take my stand
    nor swerve,
While I triumph o'er a secret wrung from nature's
    close reserve,
In you come with your cold music till I creep thro'
    every nerve.

Yes, you, like a ghostly cricket, creaking where a house
    was burned:
'Dust and ashes, dead and done with, Venice spent
    what Venice earned.
'The soul, doubtless, is immortal – where a soul can
    be discerned.

'Yours for instance: you know physics, something
        of geology,
'Mathematics are your pastime; souls shall rise in
        their degree;
'Butterflies may dread extinction, – you'll not die,
        it cannot be!

'As for Venice and her people, merely born to bloom
        and drop,
'Here on earth they bore their fruitage, mirth and folly
        were the crop:
'What of soul was left, I wonder, when the kissing had
        to stop?

'Dust and ashes!' So you creak it, and I want the heart
        to scold.
Dear dead women, with such hair, too – what's become
        of all the gold
Used to hang and brush their bosoms? I feel chilly and
        grown old.

LOVE AMONG THE RUINS

Where the quiet-coloured end of evening smiles,
   Miles and miles
On the solitary pastures where our sheep
   Half-asleep
Tinkle homeward thro' the twilight, stray or stop
   As they crop –
Was the site once of a city great and gay,
   (So they say)
Of our country's very capital, its prince
   Ages since
Held his court in, gathered councils, wielding far
   Peace or war.

Now, – the country does not even boast a tree,
   As you see,
To distinguish slopes of verdure, certain rills
   From the hills
Intersect and give a name to, (else they run
   Into one)
Where the domed and daring palace shot its spires
   Up like fires
O'er the hundred-gated circuit of a wall
   Bounding all,
Made of marble, men might march on nor be pressed,
   Twelve abreast.

And such plenty and perfection, see, of grass
        Never was!
Such a carpet as, this summer-time, o'erspreads
        And embeds
Every vestige of the city, guessed alone,
        Stock or stone –
Where a multitude of men breathed joy and woe
        Long ago;
Lust of glory pricked their hearts up, dread of shame
        Struck them tame;
And that glory and that shame alike, the gold
        Bought and sold.

Now, – the single little turret that remains
        On the plains,
By the caper overrooted, by the gourd
        Overscored,
While the patching houseleek's head of blossom winks
        Through the chinks –
Marks the basement whence a tower in ancient time
        Sprang sublime,
And a burning ring, all round, the chariots traced
        As they raced,
And the monarch and his minions and his dames
        Viewed the games.

And I know, while thus the quiet-coloured eve
        Smiles to leave
To their folding, all our many-tinkling fleece
        In such peace,
And the slopes and rills in undistinguished grey
        Melt away –
That a girl with eager eyes and yellow hair
        Waits me there
In the turret whence the charioteers caught soul
        For the goal,
When the king looked, where she looks now,
      breathless, dumb
        Till I come.

But he looked upon the city, every side,
        Far and wide,
All the mountains topped with temples, all the glades'
        Colonnades,
All the causeys, bridges, aqueducts, – and then,
        All the men!
When I do come, she will speak not, she will stand,
        Either hand
On my shoulder, give her eyes the first embrace
        Of my face,
Ere we rush, ere we extinguish sight and speech
        Each on each.

In one year they sent a million fighters forth
                    South and North,
And they built their gods a brazen pillar high
                    As the sky,
Yet reserved a thousand chariots in full force –
                    Gold, of course.
Oh heart! oh blood that freezes, blood that burns!
                    Earth's returns
For whole centuries of folly, noise and sin!
                    Shut them in,
With their triumphs and their glories and the rest!
                    Love is best.

TWO IN THE CAMPAGNA

I wonder do you feel to-day
    As I have felt since, hand in hand,
We sat down on the grass, to stray
    In spirit better through the land,
This morn of Rome and May?

For me, I touched a thought, I know,
    Has tantalized me many times,
(Like turns of thread the spiders throw
    Mocking across our path) for rhymes
To catch at and let go.

Help me to hold it! First it left
    The yellowing fennel, run to seed
There, branching from the brickwork's cleft,
    Some old tomb's ruin: yonder weed
Took up the floating weft,

Where one small orange cup amassed
    Five beetles, – blind and green they grope
Among the honey-meal: and last,
    Everywhere on the grassy slope
I traced it. Hold it fast!

The champaign with its endless fleece
    Of feathery grasses everywhere!
Silence and passion, joy and peace,
    An everlasting wash of air –
Rome's ghost since her decease.

Such life here, through such lengths of hours,
    Such miracles performed in play,
Such primal naked forms of flowers,
    Such letting nature have her way
While heaven looks from its towers!

How say you? Let us, O my dove,
    Let us be unashamed of soul,
As earth lies bare to heaven above!
    How is it under our control
To love or not to love?

I would that you were all to me,
    You that are just so much, no more.
Nor yours nor mine, nor slave nor free!
    Where does the fault lie? What the core
O' the wound, since wound must be?

I would I could adopt your will,
    See with your eyes, and set my heart
Beating by yours, and drink my fill
    At your soul's springs, – your part my part
In life, for good and ill.

No. I yearn upward, touch you close,
    Then stand away. I kiss your cheek,
Catch your soul's warmth, – I pluck the rose
    And love it more than tongue can speak –
Then the good minute goes.

Already how am I so far
    Out of that minute? Must I go
Still like the thistle-ball, no bar,
    Onward, whenever light winds blow,
Fixed by no friendly star?

Just when I seemed about to learn!
    Where is the thread now? Off again!
The old trick! Only I discern –
    Infinite passion, and the pain
Of finite hearts that yearn.

'DE GUSTIBUS –'

Your ghost will walk, you lover of trees,
  (If our loves remain)
  In an English lane,
By a cornfield-side a-flutter with poppies.
Hark, those two in the hazel coppice –
A boy and a girl, if the good fates please,
  Making love, say, –
  The happier they!
Draw yourself up from the light of the moon,
And let them pass, as they will too soon,
  With the bean-flowers' boon,
  And the blackbird's tune,
  And May, and June!

What I love best in all the world
Is a castle, precipice-encurled,
In a gash of the wind-grieved Apennine
Or look for me, old fellow of mine,
(If I get my head from out the mouth
O' the grave, and loose my spirit's bands,
And come again to the land of lands) –
In a sea-side house to the farther South,
Where the baked cicala dies of drouth,
And one sharp tree – 'tis a cypress – stands,
By the many hundred years red-rusted,

Rough iron-spiked, ripe fruit-o'ercrusted,
My sentinel to guard the sands
To the water's edge. For, what expands
Before the house, but the great opaque
Blue breadth of sea without a break?
While, in the house, for ever crumbles
Some fragment of the frescoed walls,
From blisters where a scorpion sprawls.
A girl bare-footed brings, and tumbles
Down on the pavement, green-flesh melons,
And says there's news to-day – the king
Was shot at, touched in the liver-wing,
Goes with his Bourbon arm in a sling:
– She hopes they have not caught the felons.
Italy, my Italy!
Queen Mary's saying serves for me –
         (When fortune's malice
         Lost her – Calais) –
Open my heart and you will see
Graved inside of it, 'Italy.'
Such lovers old are I and she:
So it always was, so shall ever be!

A LIGHT WOMAN

So far as our story approaches the end,
    Which do you pity the most of us three? –
My friend, or the mistress of my friend
    With her wanton eyes, or me?

My friend was already too good to lose,
    And seemed in the way of improvement yet,
When she crossed his path with her hunting-noose
    And over him drew her net.

When I saw him tangled in her toils,
    A shame, said I, if she adds just him
To her nine-and-ninety other spoils,
    The hundredth for a whim!

And before my friend be wholly hers,
    How easy to prove to him, I said,
An eagle's the game her pride prefers,
    Though she snaps at a wren instead!

So, I gave her eyes my own eyes to take,
    My hand sought hers as in earnest need,
And round she turned for my noble sake,
    And gave me herself indeed.

The eagle am I, with my fame in the world,
    The wren is he, with his maiden face.
– You look away and your lip is curled?
    Patience, a moment's space!

For see, my friend goes shaking and white;
    He eyes me as the basilisk:
I have turned, it appears, his day to night,
    Eclipsing his sun's disk.

And I did it, he thinks, as a very thief:
    'Though I love her – that, he comprehends –
'One should master one's passions, (love, in chief)
    'And be loyal to one's friends!'

And she, – she lies in my hand as tame
    As a pear late basking over a wall;
Just a touch to try and off it came;
    'Tis mine, – can I let it fall?

With no mind to eat it, that's the worst!
    Were it thrown in the road, would the case assist?
'Twas quenching a dozen blue-flies' thirst
    When I gave its stalk a twist.

And I, – what I seem to my friend, you see:
    What I soon shall seem to his love, you guess:
What I seem to myself, do you ask of me?
    No hero, I confess.

'Tis an awkward thing to play with souls,
    And matter enough to save one's own:
Yet think of my friend, and the burning coals
    He played with for bits of stone!

One likes to show the truth for the truth;
    That the woman was light is very true:
But suppose she says, – Never mind that youth!
    What wrong have I done to you?

Well, any how, here the story stays,
    So far at least as I understand;
And, Robert Browning, you writer of plays,
    Here's a subject made to your hand!

IN THREE DAYS

So, I shall see her in three days
And just one night, but nights are short,
Then two long hours, and that is morn.
See how I come, unchanged, unworn!
Feel, where my life broke off from thine,
How fresh the splinters keep and fine, –
Only a touch and we combine!

Too long, this time of year, the days!
But nights, at least the nights are short.
As night shows where her one moon is,
A hand's-breadth of pure light and bliss,
So life's night gives my lady birth
And my eyes hold her! What is worth
The rest of heaven, the rest of earth?

O loaded curls, release your store
Of warmth and scent, as once before
The tingling hair did, lights and darks
Outbreaking into fairy sparks,
When under curl and curl I pried
After the warmth and scent inside,
Thro' lights and darks how manifold –
The dark inspired, the light controlled!
As early Art embrowns the gold.

What great fear, should one say, 'Three days
'That change the world might change as well
'Your fortune; and if joy delays,
'Be happy that no worse befell!'
What small fear, if another says,
'Three days and one short night beside
'May throw no shadow on your ways;
'But years must teem with change untried,
'With chance not easily defied,
'With an end somewhere undescried.'
No fear! – or if a fear be born
This minute, it dies out in scorn.
Fear? I shall see her in three days
And one night, now the nights are short,
Then just two hours, and that is morn.

IN A YEAR

Never any more,
     While I live,
Need I hope to see his face
     As before.
Once his love grown chill,
     Mine may strive:
Bitterly we re-embrace,
     Single still.

Was it something said,
     Something done,
Vexed him? was it touch of hand,
     Turn of head?
Strange! that very way
     Love begun:
I as little understand
     Love's decay.

When I sewed or drew,
     I recall
How he looked as if I sung,
     – Sweetly too.
If I spoke a word,
     First of all
Up his cheek the colour sprung,
     Then he heard.

Sitting by my side,
    At my feet,
So he breathed but air I breathed,
    Satisfied!
I, too, at love's brim
    Touched the sweet:
I would die if death bequeathed
    Sweet to him.

'Speak, I love thee best!'
    He exclaimed:
'Let thy love my own foretell!'
    I confessed:
'Clasp my heart on thine
    'Now unblamed,
'Since upon thy soul as well
    'Hangeth mine!'

Was it wrong to own,
    Being truth?
Why should all the giving prove
    His alone?
I had wealth and ease,
    Beauty, youth:
Since my lover gave me love,
    I gave these.

That was all I meant,
    – To be just,
And the passion I had raised,
    To content.
Since he chose to change
    Gold for dust,
If I gave him what he praised
    Was it strange?

Would he loved me yet,
    On and on,
While I found some way undreamed
    – Paid my debt!
Gave more life and more,
    Till, all gone,
He should smile 'She never seemed
    'Mine before.

'What, she felt the while,
    'Must I think?
'Love's so different with us men!'
    He should smile:
'Dying for my sake –
    'White and pink!
'Can't we touch these bubbles then
    'But they break?'

Dear, the pang is brief,
    Do thy part,
Have thy pleasure! How perplexed
    Grows belief!
Well, this cold clay clod
    Was man's heart:
Crumble it, and what comes next?
    Is it God?

TIME'S REVENGES

I've a Friend, over the sea;
I like him, but he loves me.
It all grew out of the books I write;
They find such favour in his sight
That he slaughters you with savage looks
Because you don't admire my books.
He does himself though, – and if some vein
Were to snap to-night in this heavy brain,
To-morrow month, if I lived to try,
Round should I just turn quietly,
Or out of the bedclothes stretch my hand
Till I found him, come from his foreign land
To be my nurse in this poor place,
And make my broth and wash my face
And light my fire and, all the while,
Bear with his old good-humoured smile
That I told him 'Better have kept away
'Than come and kill me, night and day,
'With, worse than fever throbs and shoots,
'The creaking of his clumsy boots.'
I am as sure that this he would do,
As that Saint Paul's is striking two.
And I think I rather... woe is me!
– Yes, rather would see him than not see,
If lifting a hand could seat him there

Before me in the empty chair
To-night, when my head aches indeed,
And I can neither think nor read
Nor make these purple fingers hold
The pen; this garret's freezing cold!

And I've a Lady – there he wakes,
The laughing fiend and prince of snakes
Within me, at her name, to pray
Fate send some creature in the way
Of my love for her, to be down-torn,
Upthrust and outward-borne,
So I might prove myself that sea
Of passion which I needs must be!
Call my thoughts false and my fancies quaint
And my style infirm and its figures faint,
All the critics say, and more blame yet,
And not one angry word you get.
But, please you, wonder I would put
My cheek beneath that lady's foot
Rather than trample under mine
The laurels of the Florentine,
And you shall see how the devil spends
A fire God gave for other ends!
I tell you, I stride up and down

This garret, crowned with love's best crown,
And feasted with love's perfect feast,
To think I kill for her, at least,
Body and soul and peace and fame,
Alike youth's end and manhood's aim,
– So is my spirit, as flesh with sin,
Filled full, eaten out and in
With the face of her, the eyes of her,
The lips, the little chin, the stir
Of shadow round her mouth; and she
– I'll tell you, – calmly would decree
That I should roast at a slow fire,
If that would compass her desire
And make her one whom they invite
To the famous ball to-morrow night.

There may be heaven; there must be hell;
Meantime, there is our earth here – well!

POPULARITY

Stand still, true poet that you are!
   I know you; let me try and draw you.
Some night you'll fail us: when afar
   You rise, remember one man saw you,
Knew you, and named a star!

My star, God's glow-worm! Why extend
   That loving hand of his which leads you
Yet locks you safe from end to end
   Of this dark world, unless he needs you,
Just saves your light to spend?

His clenched hand shall unclose at last,
   I know, and let out all the beauty:
My poet holds the future fast,
   Accepts the coming ages' duty,
Their present for this past.

That day, the earth's feast-master's brow
   Shall clear, to God the chalice raising;
'Others give best at first, but thou
   'Forever set'st our table praising,
'Keep'st the good wine till now!'

Meantime, I'll draw you as you stand,
  With few or none to watch and wonder:
I'll say – a fisher, on the sand
  By Tyre the old, with ocean-plunder,
A netful, brought to land.

Who has not heard how Tyrian shells
  Enclosed the blue, that dye of dyes
Whereof one drop worked miracles,
  And coloured like Astarte's eyes
Raw silk the merchant sells?

And each bystander of them all
  Could criticize, and quote tradition
How depths of blue sublimed some pall
  – To get which, pricked a king's ambition;
Worth sceptre, crown and ball.

Yet there's the dye, in that rough mesh,
  The sea has only just o'erwhispered!
Live whelks, each lip's beard dripping fresh,
  As if they still the water's lisp heard
Through foam the rock-weeds thresh.

Enough to furnish Solomon
  Such hangings for his cedar-house,
That, when gold-robed he took the throne

In that abyss of blue, the Spouse
Might swear his presence shone

Most like the centre-spike of gold
    Which burns deep in the blue-bell's womb,
What time, with ardours manifold,
    The bee goes singing to her groom,
Drunken and overbold.

Mere conchs! not fit for warp or woof!
    Till cunning come to pound and squeeze
And clarify, – refine to proof
    The liquor filtered by degrees,
While the world stands aloof.

And there's the extract, flasked and fine,
    And priced and saleable at last!
And Hobbs, Nobbs, Stokes and Nokes combine
    To paint the future from the past,
Put blue into their line.

Hobbs hints blue, – straight he turtle eats:
    Nobbs prints blue, – claret crowns his cup:
Nokes outdares Stokes in azure feats, –
    Both gorge. Who fished the murex up?
What porridge had John Keats?

MEMORABILIA

Ah, did you once see Shelley plain,
   And did he stop and speak to you
And did you speak to him again?
   How strange it seems and new!

But you were living before that,
   And also you are living after;
And the memory I started at –
   My starting moves your laughter.

I crossed a moor, with a name of its own
   And a certain use in the world no doubt,
Yet a hand's-breadth of it shines alone
   'Mid the blank miles round about:

For there I picked up on the heather
   And there I put inside my breast
A moulted feather, an eagle-feather!
   Well, I forget the rest.

HOW IT STRIKES A CONTEMPORARY

I only knew one poet in my life:
And this, or something like it, was his way.

    You saw go up and down Valladolid,
A man of mark, to know next time you saw.
His very serviceable suit of black
Was courtly once and conscientious still,
And many might have worn it, though none did:
The cloak, that somewhat shone and showed the
        threads,
Had purpose, and the ruff, significance.
He walked and tapped the pavement with his cane,
Scenting the world, looking it full in face,
An old dog, bald and blindish, at his heels.
They turned up, now, the alley by the church,
That leads nowhither; now, they breathed themselves
On the main promenade just at the wrong time:
You'd come upon his scrutinizing hat,
Making a peaked shade blacker than itself
Against the single window spared some house
Intact yet with its mouldered Moorish work, –
Or else surprise the ferrel of his stick
Trying the mortar's temper 'tween the chinks
Of some new shop a-building, French and fine.
He stood and watched the cobbler at his trade,

The man who slices lemons into drink,
The coffee-roaster's brazier, and the boys
That volunteer to help him turn its winch.
He glanced o'er books on stalls with half an eye,
And fly-leaf ballads on the vendor's string,
And broad-edge bold-print posters by the wall.
He took such cognizance of men and things,
If any beat a horse, you felt he saw;
If any cursed a woman, he took note;
Yet stared at nobody, – you stared at him,
And found, less to your pleasure than surprise,
He seemed to know you and expect as much.
So, next time that a neighbour's tongue was loosed,
It marked the shameful and notorious fact,
We had among us, not so much a spy,
As a recording chief-inquisitor,
The town's true master if the town but knew!
We merely kept a governor for form,
While this man walked about and took account
Of all thought, said and acted, then went home,
And wrote it fully to our Lord the King
Who has an itch to know things, he knows why,
And reads them in his bedroom of a night.
Oh, you might smile! there wanted not a touch,
A tang of . . . well, it was not wholly ease
As back into your mind the man's look came.
Stricken in years a little, – such a brow

His eyes had to live under! – clear as flint
On either side the formidable nose
Curved, cut and coloured like an eagle's claw.
Had he to do with A.'s surprising fate?
When altogether old B. disappeared
And young C. got his mistress, – was't our friend,
His letter to the King, that did it all?
What paid the bloodless man for so much pains?
Our Lord the King has favourites manifold,
And shifts his ministry some once a month;
Our city gets new governors at whiles, –
But never word or sign, that I could hear,
Notified to this man about the streets
The King's approval of those letters conned
The last thing duly at the dead of night.
Did the man love his office? Frowned our Lord,
Exhorting when none heard – 'Beseech me not!
'Too far above my people, – beneath me!
'I set the watch, – how should the people know?
'Forget them, keep me all the more in mind!'
Was some such understanding 'twixt the two?

    I found no truth in one report at least –
That if you tracked him to his home, down lanes
Beyond the Jewry, and as clean to pace,
You found he ate his supper in a room
Blazing with lights, four Titians on the wall,

And twenty naked girls to change his plate!
Poor man, he lived another kind of life
In that new stuccoed third house by the bridge,
Fresh-painted, rather smart than otherwise!
The whole street might o'erlook him as he sat,
Leg crossing leg, one foot on the dog's back,
Playing a decent cribbage with his maid
(Jacynth, you're sure her name was) o'er the cheese
And fruit, three red halves of starved winter-pears,
Or treat of radishes in April. Nine,
Ten, struck the church clock, straight to bed went he.

My father, like the man of sense he was,
Would point him out to me a dozen times;
''St – 'St,' he'd whisper, 'the Corregidor!'
I had been used to think that personage
Was one with lacquered breeches, lustrous belt,
And feathers like a forest in his hat,
Who blew a trumpet and proclaimed the news,
Announced the bull-fights, gave each church its turn,
And memorized the miracle in vogue!
He had a great observance from us boys;
We were in error; that was not the man.

I'd like now, yet had haply been afraid,
To have just looked, when this man came to die,
And seen who lined the clean gay garret-sides

And stood about the neat low truckle-bed,
With the heavenly manner of relieving guard.
Here had been, mark, the general-in-chief,
Thro' a whole campaign of the world's life and death,
Doing the King's work all the dim day long,
In his old coat and up to knees in mud,
Smoked like a herring, dining on a crust, –
And, now the day was won, relieved at once!
No further show or need for that old coat,
You are sure, for one thing! Bless us, all the while
How sprucely we are dressed out, you and I!
A second, and the angels alter that.
Well, I could never write a verse, – could you?
Let's to the Prado and make the most of time.

MY STAR

All that I know
  Of a certain star
Is, it can throw
  (Like the angled spar)
Now a dart of red,
  Now a dart of blue;
Till my friends have said
  They would fain see, too,
My star that dartles the red and the blue!
Then it stops like a bird; like a flower, hangs furled:
  They must solace themselves with the Saturn above it.
What matter to me if their star is a world?
  Mine has opened its soul to me; therefore I love it.

FAME

See, as the prettiest graves will do in time,
Our poet's wants the freshness of its prime;
Spite of the sexton's browsing horse, the sods
Have struggled through its binding osier rods;
Headstone and half-sunk footstone lean awry,
Wanting the brick-work promised by-and-by;
How the minute grey lichens, plate o'er plate,
Have softened down the crisp-cut name and date!

THE LOST LEADER

Just for a handful of silver he left us,
  Just for a riband to stick in his coat –
Found the one gift of which fortune bereft us,
  Lost all the others she lets us devote;
They, with the gold to give, doled him out silver,
  So much was theirs who so little allowed:
How all our copper had gone for his service!
  Rags – were they purple, his heart had been proud!
We that had loved him so, followed him, honoured him,
  Lived in his mild and magnificent eye,
Learned his great language, caught his clear accents,
  Made him our pattern to live and to die!
Shakespeare was of us, Milton was for us,
  Burns, Shelley, were with us, – they watch from
    their graves!
He alone breaks from the van and the freemen,
  – He alone sinks to the rear and the slaves!

We shall march prospering, – not thro' his presence;
  Songs may inspirit us, – not from his lyre;
Deeds will be done, – while he boasts his quiescence,
  Still bidding crouch whom the rest bade aspire:
Blot out his name, then, record one lost soul more,
  One task more declined, one more footpath untrod,
One more devils'-triumph and sorrow for angels,

One wrong more to man, one more insult to God!
Life's night begins: let him never come back to us!
    There would be doubt, hesitation and pain,
Forced praise on our part – the glimmer of twilight,
    Never glad confident morning again!
Best fight on well, for we taught him – strike gallantly,
    Menace our heart ere we master his own;
Then let him receive the new knowledge and wait us,
    Pardoned in heaven, the first by the throne!

MISCONCEPTIONS

This is a spray the Bird clung to,
    Making it blossom with pleasure,
Ere the high tree-top she sprung to,
    Fit for her nest and her treasure.
    Oh, what a hope beyond measure
Was the poor spray's, which the flying feet hung to, –
So to be singled out, built in, and sung to!

This is a heart the Queen leant on,
    Thrilled in a minute erratic,
Ere the true bosom she bent on,
    Meet for love's regal dalmatic.
    Oh, what a fancy ecstatic
Was the poor heart's, ere the wanderer went on –
    Love to be saved for it, proffered to, spent on!

INAPPREHENSIVENESS

We two stood simply friend-like side by side,
Viewing a twilight country far and wide,
Till she at length broke silence. 'How it towers
Yonder, the ruin o'er this vale of ours!
The West's faint flare behind it so relieves
Its rugged outline – sight perhaps deceives,
Or I could almost fancy that I see
A branch wave plain – belike some wind-sown tree
Chance-rooted where a missing turret was.
What would I give for the perspective glass
At home, to make out if 'tis really so!
Has Ruskin noticed here at Asolo
That certain weed-growths on the ravaged wall
Seem' ... something that I could not say at all,
My thought being rather – as absorbed she sent
Look onward after look from eyes distent
With longing to reach Heaven's gate left ajar –
'Oh, fancies that might be, oh, facts that are!
What of a wilding? By you stands, and may
So stand unnoticed till the Judgment Day,
One who, if once aware that your regard
Claimed what his heart holds, – woke, as from
    its sward
The flower, the dormant passion, so to speak –
Then what a rush of life would startling wreak

Revenge on your inapprehensive stare
While, from the ruin and the West's faint flare,
You let your eyes meet mine, touch what you term
Quietude – that's an universe in germ –
The dormant passion needing but a look
To burst into immense life!'
                                    'No, the book
Which noticed how the wall-growths wave' said she
'Was not by Ruskin.'
                                    I said 'Vernon Lee?'

DUBIETY

I will be happy if but for once:
    Only help me, Autumn weather,
Me and my cares to screen, ensconce
    In luxury's sofa-lap of leather!

Sleep? Nay, comfort – with just a cloud
    Suffusing day too clear and bright:
Eve's essence, the single drop allowed
    To sully, like milk, Noon's water-white.

Let gauziness shade, not shroud, – adjust,
    Dim and not deaden, – somehow sheathe
Aught sharp in the rough world's busy thrust,
    If it reach me through dreaming's vapour-wreath.

Be life so, all things ever the same!
    For, what has disarmed the world? Outside,
Quiet and peace: inside, nor blame
    Nor want, nor wish whate'er betide.

What is it like that has happened before?
    A dream? No dream, more real by much.
A vision? But fanciful days of yore
    Brought many: mere musing seems not such.

Perhaps but a memory, after all!
    – Of what came once when a woman leant
To feel for my brow where her kiss might fall.
    Truth ever, truth only the excellent!

RESPECTABILITY

Dear, had the world in its caprice
    Deigned to proclaim 'I know you both,
    'Have recognized your plighted troth,
'Am sponsor for you: live in peace!' –
How many precious months and years
    Of youth had passed, that speed so fast,
    Before we found it out at last,
The world, and what it fears?

How much of priceless life were spent
    With men that every virtue decks,
    And women models of their sex,
Society's true ornament, –
Ere we dared wander, nights like this,
    Thro' wind and rain, and watch the Seine,
    And feel the Boulevard break again
To warmth and light and bliss?

I know! the world proscribes not love;
    Allows my finger to caress
    Your lips' contour and downiness,
Provided it supply a glove.
The world's good word! – the Institute!
    Guizot receives Montalembert!
    Eh? Down the court three lampions flare:
Put forward your best foot!

HUMILITY

What girl but, having gathered flowers,
Stript the beds and spoilt the bowers,
From the lapful light she carries
Drops a careless bud? – nor tarries
To regain the waif and stray:
 'Store enough for home' – she'll say.

So say I too: give your lover
Heaps of loving – under, over,
Whelm him – make the one the wealthy!
Am I all so poor who – stealthy
Work it was! – picked up what fell:
Not the worst bud – who can tell?

SUMMUM BONUM

All the breath and the bloom of the year in
    the bag of one bee:
  All the wonder and wealth of the mine in
    the heart of one gem:
In the core of one pearl all the shade and the
    shine of the sea:
  Breath and bloom, shade and shine, – won-
    der, wealth, and – how far above them –
      Truth, that's brighter than gem,
      Trust, that's purer than pearl, –
Brightest truth, purest trust in the universe –
    all were for me
      In the kiss of one girl.

SPECULATIVE

Others may need new life in Heaven –
    Man, Nature, Art – made new, assume!
Man with new mind old sense to leaven,
    Nature – new light to clear old gloom,
Art that breaks bounds, gets soaring-room.

I shall pray: 'Fugitive as precious –
    Minutes which passed, – return, remain!
Let earth's old life once more enmesh us,
    You with old pleasure, me – old pain,
So we but meet nor part again!'

IN THE DOORWAY
From JAMES LEE'S WIFE

The swallow has set her six young on the rail,
    And looks sea-ward:
The water's in stripes like a snake, olive-pale
    To the leeward, –
On the weather-side, black, spotted white with
    the wind.
'Good fortune departs, and disaster's behind,' –
Hark, the wind with its wants and its infinite wail!

Our fig-tree, that leaned for the saltness, has furled
    Her five fingers,
Each leaf like a hand opened wide to the world
    Where there lingers
No glint of the gold, Summer sent for her sake:
How the vines writhe in rows, each impaled on its stake!
My heart shrivels up and my spirit shrinks curled.

Yet here are we two; we have love, house enough,
    With the field there,
This house of four rooms, that field red and rough,
    Though it yield there,
For the rabbit that robs, scarce a blade or a bent;
If a magpie alight now, it seems an event;
And they both will be gone at November's rebuff.

But why must cold spread? but wherefore bring
     change
        To the spirit,
God meant should mate his with an infinite range,
        And inherit
His power to put life in the darkness and cold?
Oh, live and love worthily, bear and be bold!
Whom Summer made friends of, let Winter estrange!

MAY AND DEATH

I wish that when you died last May,
    Charles, there had died along with you
Three parts of spring's delightful things;
    Ay, and, for me, the fourth part too.

A foolish thought, and worse, perhaps!
    There must be many a pair of friends
Who, arm in arm, deserve the warm
    Moon-births and the long evening-ends.

So, for their sake, be May still May!
    Let their new time, as mine of old,
Do all it did for me: I bid
    Sweet sights and sounds throng manifold.

Only, one little sight, one plant,
    Woods have in May, that starts up green
Save a sole streak which, so to speak,
    Is spring's blood, spilt its leaves between, –

That, they might spare; a certain wood
    Might miss the plant; their loss were small:
But I, – whene'er the leaf grows there,
    Its drop comes from my heart, that's all.

HOME-THOUGHTS, FROM ABROAD

Oh, to be in England
Now that April's there,
And whoever wakes in England
Sees, some morning, unaware,
That the lowest boughs and the brushwood sheaf
Round the elm-tree bole are in tiny leaf,
While the chaffinch sings on the orchard bough
In England – now!

And after April, when May follows,
And the whitethroat builds, and all the swallows!
Hark, where my blossomed pear-tree in the hedge
Leans to the field and scatters on the clover
Blossoms and dewdrops – at the bent spray's edge –
That's the wise thrush; he sings each song twice over,
Lest you should think he never could recapture
The first fine careless rapture!
And though the fields look rough with hoary dew,
All will be gay when noontide wakes anew
The buttercups, the little children's dower
– Far brighter than this gaudy melon-flower!

PROSPICE

Fear death? – to feel the fog in my throat,
        The mist in my face,
When the snows begin, and the blasts denote
        I am nearing the place,
The power of the night, the press of the storm,
        The post of the foe;
Where he stands, the Arch Fear in a visible form,
        Yet the strong man must go:
For the journey is done and the summit attained,
        And the barriers fall,
Though a battle's to fight ere the guerdon be gained,
        The reward of it all.

I was ever a fighter, so – one fight more,
        The best and the last!
I would hate that death bandaged my eyes and forbore,
        And bade me creep past.
No! let me taste the whole of it, fare like my peers
        The heroes of old,
Bear the brunt, in a minute pay glad life's arrears
        Of pain, darkness and cold.
For sudden the worst turns the best to the brave,
        The black minute's at end,
And the elements' rage, the fiend-voices that rave,
        Shall dwindle, shall blend,

Shall change, shall become first a peace out of pain,
  Then a light, then thy breast,
O thou soul of my soul! I shall clasp thee again,
  And with God be the rest!

A FACE

If one could have that little head of hers
    Painted upon a background of pale gold,
Such as the Tuscan's early art prefers!
    No shade encroaching on the matchless mould
Of those two lips, which should be opening soft
    In the pure profile; not as when she laughs,
For that spoils all: but rather as if aloft
    Yon hyacinth, she loves so, leaned its staff's
Burthen of honey-coloured buds to kiss
And capture 'twixt the lips apart for this.
Then her lithe neck, three fingers might surround,
How it should waver on the pale gold ground
Up to the fruit-shaped, perfect chin it lifts!
I know, Correggio loves to mass, in rifts
Of heaven, his angel faces, orb on orb
Breaking its outline, burning shades absorb:
But these are only massed there, I should think,
    Waiting to see some wonder momently
    Grow out, stand full, fade slow against the sky
    (That's the pale ground you'd see this sweet face by),
    All heaven, meanwhile, condensed into one eye
Which fears to lose the wonder, should it wink.

MAGICAL NATURE

Flower – I never fancied, jewel – I profess you!
    Bright I see and soft I feel the outside of a flower.
Save but glow inside and – jewel, I should guess you,
    Dim to sight and rough to touch: the glory is
        the dower.

You, forsooth, a flower? Nay, my love, a jewel –
    Jewel at no mercy of a moment in your prime!
Time may fray the flower-face: kind be time or cruel,
    Jewel, from each facet, flash your laugh at time!

NATURAL MAGIC

All I can say is – I saw it!
The room was as bare as your hand.
I locked in the swarth little lady, – I swear,
From the head to the foot of her – well, quite as bare!
'No Nautch shall cheat me,' said I, 'taking my stand
At this bolt which I draw!' And this bolt – I withdraw it,
And there laughs the lady, not bare, but embowered
With – who knows what verdure, o'erfruited,
    o'erflowered?
      Impossible! Only – I saw it!

      All I can sing is – I feel it!
This life was as blank as that room;
I let you pass in here. Precaution, indeed?
Walls, ceiling and floor, – not a chance for a weed!
Wide opens the entrance: where's cold now,
    where's gloom?
No May to sow seed here, no June to reveal it,
Behold you enshrined in these blooms of your
    bringing,
These fruits of your bearing – nay, birds of your
    winging!
      A fairy-tale! Only – I feel it!

WHITE WITCHCRAFT

If you and I could change to beasts, what
    beast should either be?
Shall you and I play Jove for once? Turn
    fox then, I decree!
Shy wild sweet stealer of the grapes! Now
    do your worst on me!

And thus you think to spite your friend –
    turned loathsome? What, a toad?
So, all men shrink and shun me! Dear men,
    pursue your road!
Leave but my crevice in the stone, a reptile's
    fit abode!

Now say your worst, Canidia! 'He's
    loathsome, I allow:
There may or may not lurk a pearl beneath
    his puckered brow:
But see his eyes that follow mine – love lasts
    there anyhow.'

HOUSE

Shall I sonnet-sing you about myself?
    Do I live in a house you would like to see?
Is it scant of gear, has it store of pelf?
    'Unlock my heart with a sonnet-key?'

Invite the world, as my betters have done?
    'Take notice: this building remains on view,
Its suites of reception every one,
    Its private apartment and bedroom too;

'For a ticket, apply to the Publisher.'
    No: thanking the public, I must decline.
A peep through my window, if folk prefer;
    But, please you, no foot over threshold of mine!

I have mixed with a crowd and heard free talk
    In a foreign land where an earthquake chanced:
And a house stood gaping, nought to baulk
    Man's eye wherever he gazed or glanced.

The whole of the frontage shaven sheer,
    The inside gaped: exposed to day,
Right and wrong and common and queer,
    Bare, as the palm of your hand, it lay.

The owner? Oh, he had been crushed, no doubt!
    'Odd tables and chairs for a man of wealth!
What a parcel of musty old books about!
    He smoked, – no wonder he lost his health!

'I doubt if he bathed before he dressed.
    A brasier? – the pagan, he burned perfumes!
You see it is proved, what the neighbours guessed:
    His wife and himself had separate rooms.'

Friends, the goodman of the house at least
    Kept house to himself till an earthquake came:
'Tis the fall of its frontage permits you feast
    On the inside arrangement you praise or blame.

Outside should suffice for evidence:
    And whoso desires to penetrate
Deeper, must dive by the spirit-sense –
    No optics like yours, at any rate!

'Hoity toity! A street to explore,
    Your house the exception! "*With this same key
Shakespeare unlocked his heart,*" once more!'
    Did Shakespeare? If so, the less Shakespeare he!

APPEARANCES

And so you found that poor room dull,
    Dark, hardly to your taste, my dear?
Its features seemed unbeautiful:
    But this I know – 'twas there, not here,
You plighted troth to me, the word
Which – ask that poor room how it heard.

And this rich room obtains your praise
    Unqualified, – so bright, so fair,
So all whereat perfection stays?
    Ay, but remember – here, not there,
The other word was spoken! Ask
This rich room how you dropped the mask!

ELIZABETH BARRETT BROWNING

QUESTION AND ANSWER

Love you seek for, presupposes
    Summer heat and sunny glow.
Tell me, do you find moss-roses
    Budding, blooming in the snow?
Snow might kill the rose-tree's root –
Shake it quickly from your foot,
    Lest it harm you as you go.

From the ivy where it dapples
    A grey ruin, stone by stone,
Do you look for grapes or apples,
    Or for sad green leaves alone?
Pluck the leaves off, two or three –
Keep them for mortality
    When you shall be safe and gone.

A WOMAN'S SHORTCOMINGS

She has laughed as softly as if she sighed,
   She has counted six, and over,
Of a purse well filled and a heart well tried –
   Oh, each a worthy lover!
They 'give her time;' for her soul must slip
   Where the world has set the grooving;
She will lie to none with her fair red lip:
   But love seeks truer loving.

She trembles her fan in a sweetness dumb,
   As her thoughts were beyond recalling,
With a glance for *one*, and a glance for *some*,
   From her eyelids rising and falling;
Speaks common words with a blushful air,
   Hears bold words, unreproving;
But her silence says – what she never will swear –
   And love seeks better loving.

Go, lady, lean to the night-guitar
   And drop a smile to the bringer;
Then smile as sweetly, when he is far,
   At the voice of an in-door singer.
Bask tenderly beneath tender eyes;
   Glance lightly, on their removing;
And join new vows to old perjuries –
   But dare not call it loving.

Unless you can think, when the song is done,
    No other is soft in the rhythm;
Unless you can feel, when left by One,
    That all men else go with him;
Unless you can know, when unpraised by his breath,
    That your beauty itself wants proving;
Unless you can swear 'For life, for death!' –
    Oh, fear to call it loving!

Unless you can muse in a crowd all day
    On the absent face that fixed you;
Unless you can love, as the angels may,
    With the breadth of heaven betwixt you;
Unless you can dream that his faith is fast,
    Through behoving and unbehoving;
Unless you can *die* when the dream is past –
    Oh, never call it loving!

A MAN'S REQUIREMENTS

Love me, Sweet, with all thou art,
    Feeling, thinking, seeing;
Love me in the lightest part,
    Love me in full being.

Love me with thine open youth
    In its frank surrender;
With the vowing of thy mouth,
    With its silence tender.

Love me with thine azure eyes,
    Made for earnest granting;
Taking colour from the skies,
    Can Heaven's truth be wanting?

Love me with their lids, that fall
    Snow-like at first meeting;
Love me with thine heart, that all
    Neighbours then see beating.

Love me with thine hand stretched out
    Freely – open-minded;
Love me with thy loitering foot, –
    Hearing one behind it.

Love me with thy voice, that turns
    Sudden faint above me;

Love me with thy blush that burns
    When I murmur *Love me!*

Love me with thy thinking soul,
    Break it to love-sighing;
Love me with thy thoughts that roll
    On through living – dying.

Love me in thy gorgeous airs,
    When the world has crowned thee;
Love me, kneeling at thy prayers,
    With the angels round thee.

Love me pure, as musers do,
    Up the woodlands shady:
Love me gaily, fast and true,
    As a winsome lady.

Through all hopes that keep us brave,
    Farther off or nigher,
Love me for the house and grave,
    And for something higher.

Thus, if thou wilt prove me, Dear,
    Woman's love no fable,
I will love *thee* – half a year –
    As a man is able.

A SEA-SIDE WALK

We walked beside the sea
After a day which perished silently
Of its own glory – like the princess weird
Who, combating the Genius, scorched and seared,
Uttered with burning breath, 'Ho! victory!'
And sank adown, a heap of ashes pale:
    So runs the Arab tale.

The sky above us showed
A universal and unmoving cloud
On which the cliffs permitted us to see
Only the outline of their majesty,
As master-minds when gazed at by the crowd:
And shining with a gloom, the water grey
    Swang in its moon-taught way.

Nor moon, nor stars were out;
They did not dare to tread so soon about,
Though trembling, in the footsteps of the sun:
The light was neither night's nor day's, but one
Which, life-like, had a beauty in its doubt.
And silence's impassioned breathings round
    Seemed wandering into sound.

O solemn-beating heart
Of nature! I have knowledge that thou art
Bound unto man's by cords he cannot sever;
And, what time they are slackened by him ever,
So to attest his own supernal part,
Still runneth thy vibration fast and strong
　　The slackened cord along:

　　For though we never spoke
Of the grey water and the shaded rock,
Dark wave and stone unconsciously were fused
Into the plaintive speaking that we used
Of absent friends and memories unforsook;
And, had we seen each other's face, we had
　　Seen haply each was sad.

TO FLUSH, MY DOG

Loving friend, the gift of one
Who her own true faith has run
   Through thy lower nature,
Be my benediction said
With my hand upon thy head,
   Gentle fellow-creature!

Like a lady's ringlets brown,
Flow thy silken ears adown
   Either side demurely
Of thy silver-suited breast
Shining out from all the rest
   Of thy body purely.

Darkly brown thy body is,
Till the sunshine striking this
   Alchemize its dullness,
When the sleek curls manifold
Flash all over into gold
   With a burnished fullness.

Underneath my stroking hand,
Startled eyes of hazel bland
   Kindling, growing larger,
Up thou leapest with a spring,
Full of prank and curveting,
   Leaping like a charger.

Leap! thy broad tail waves a light,
Leap! thy slender feet are bright,
    Canopied in fringes;
Leap! those tasselled ears of thine
Flicker strangely, fair and fine
    Down their golden inches.

Yet, my pretty, sportive friend,
Little is't to such an end
    That I praise thy rareness;
Other dogs may be thy peers
Haply in these drooping ears
    And this glossy fairness.

But of *thee* it shall be said,
This dog watched beside a bed
    Day and night unweary,
Watched within a curtained room
Where no sunbeam brake the gloom
    Round the sick and dreary.

Roses, gathered for a vase,
In that chamber died apace,
    Beam and breeze resigning;
This dog only, waited on,
Knowing that when light is gone
    Love remains for shining.

Other dogs in thymy dew
Tracked the hares and followed through
   Sunny moor or meadow;
This dog only, crept and crept
Next a languid cheek that slept,
   Sharing in the shadow.

Other dogs of loyal cheer
Bounded at the whistle clear,
   Up the woodside hieing;
This dog only, watched in reach
Of a faintly uttered speech
   Or a louder sighing.

And if one or two quick tears
Dropped upon his glossy ears
   Or a sigh came double,
Up he sprang in eager haste,
Fawning, fondling, breathing fast,
   In a tender trouble.

And this dog was satisfied
If a pale thin hand would glide
   Down his dewlaps sloping, –
Which he pushed his nose within,
After, – platforming his chin
   On the palm left open.

This dog, if a friendly voice
Call him now to blither choice
   Than such chamber-keeping,
'Come out!' praying from the door, –
Presseth backward as before,
   Up against me leaping.

Therefore to this dog will I,
Tenderly not scornfully,
   Render praise and favour:
With my hand upon his head,
Is my benediction said
   Therefore and for ever.

And because he loves me so,
Better than his kind will do
   Often man or woman,
Give I back more love again
Than dogs often take of men,
   Leaning from my Human.

Blessings on thee, dog of mine,
Pretty collars make thee fine,
   Sugared milk make fat thee!
Pleasures wag on in thy tail,
Hands of gentle motion fail
   Nevermore, to pat thee!

Downy pillow take thy head,
Silken coverlid bestead,
    Sunshine help thy sleeping!
No fly's buzzing wake thee up,
No man break thy purple cup
    Set for drinking deep in.

Whiskered cats arointed flee,
Sturdy stoppers keep from thee
    Cologne distillations;
Nuts lie in thy path for stones,
And thy feast-day macaroons
    Turn to daily rations!

Mock I thee, in wishing weal? –
Tears are in my eyes to feel
    Thou art made so straitly,
Blessing needs must straiten too, –
Little canst thou joy or do,
    Thou who lovest *greatly*.

Yet be blessèd to the height
Of all good and all delight
    Pervious to thy nature;
Only *loved* beyond that line,
With a love that answers thine,
    Loving fellow-creature!

FLUSH OR FAUNUS

You see this dog. It was but yesterday
I mused, forgetful of his presence here,
Till thought on thought drew downward tear on tear;
When from the pillow, where wet-checked I lay,
A head as hairy as Faunus, thrust its way
Right sudden against my face, – two golden-clear
Large eyes astonished mine, – a drooping ear
Did flap me on either cheek, to dry the spray!
I started first, as some Arcadian
Amazed by goatly god in twilight grove:
But as my bearded vision closelier ran
My tears off, I knew Flush, and rose above
Surprise and sadness; thanking the true PAN,
Who, by low creatures, leads to heights of love.

GRIEF

I tell you, hopeless grief is passionless;
That only men incredulous of despair,
Half-taught in anguish, through the midnight air
Beat upward to God's throne in loud access
Of shrieking and reproach. Full desertness,
In souls as countries, lieth, silent-bare
Under the blanching, vertical eye-glare
Of the absolute Heavens. Deep-hearted man, express
Grief for thy Dead in silence like to death –
Most like a monumental statue set
In everlasting watch and moveless woe
Till itself crumble to the dust beneath.
Touch it; the marble eyelids are not wet:
If it could weep, it could arise and go.

DISCONTENT

Light human nature is too lightly tost
And ruffled without cause, complaining on –
Restless with rest, until, being overthrown,
It learneth to lie quiet. Let a frost
Or a small wasp have crept to the innermost
Of our ripe peach, or let the wilful sun
Shine westward of our window, – straight we run
A furlong's sigh as if the world were lost.
But what time through the heart and through the brain
God hath transfixed us, – we, so moved before,
Attain to a calm. Ay, shouldering weights of pain,
We anchor in deep waters, safe from shore,
And hear submissive o'er the stormy main
God's chartered judgements walk for evermore.

PATIENCE TAUGHT BY NATURE

'O dreary life,' we cry, 'O dreary life!'
And still the generations of the birds
Sing through our sighing, and the flocks and herds
Serenely live while we are keeping strife
With Heaven's true purpose in us, as a knife
Against which we may struggle! Ocean girds
Unslackened the dry land, savannah-swards
Unweary sweep, hills watch unworn, and rife
Meek leaves drop yearly from the forest-trees
To show, above, the unwasted stars that pass
In their old glory: O thou God of old,
Grant me some smaller grace than comes to these! –
But so much patience as a blade of grass
Grows by, contented through the heat and cold.

THE WEAKEST THING

Which is the weakest thing of all
    Mine heart can ponder?
The sun, a little cloud can pall
    With darkness yonder?
The cloud, a little wind can move
    Where'er it listeth?
The wind, a little leaf above,
    Though sere, resisteth?

What time that yellow leaf was green,
    My days were gladder;
But now, whatever Spring may mean,
    I must grow sadder.
Ah me! a *leaf* with sighs can wring
    My lips asunder –
Then is mine heart the weakest thing
    Itself can ponder.

Yet, Heart, when sun and cloud are pined,
    And drop together,
And at a blast which is not wind,
    The forests wither,
Thou, from the darkening deathly curse,
    To glory breakest, –
The Strongest of the universe
    Guarding the weakest!

A DEAD ROSE

O Rose, who dares to name thee?
No longer roseate now, nor soft nor sweet,
But pale and hard and dry as stubble wheat, –
    Kept seven years in a drawer, thy titles shame thee.

The breeze that used to blow thee
Between the hedgerow thorns, and take away
An odour up the lane to last all day, –
    If breathing now, unsweetened would forgo thee.

The sun that used to smite thee,
And mix his glory in thy gorgeous urn
Till beam appeared to bloom, and flower to burn, –
    If shining now, with not a hue would light thee.

The dew that used to wet thee,
And, white first, grow incarnadined because
It lay upon thee where the crimson was, –
    If dropping now, would darken where it met thee.

The fly that 'lit upon thee
To stretch the tendrils of its tiny feet
Along thy leaf's pure edges after heat, –
    If 'lighting now, would coldly overrun thee.

The bee that once did suck thee,
And build thy perfumed ambers up his hive,
And swoon in thee for joy, till scarce alive, –
   If passing now, would blindly overlook thee.

The heart doth recognize thee,
Alone, alone! the heart doth smell thee sweet,
Doth view thee fair, doth judge thee most complete,
   Perceiving all those changes that disguise thee.

Yes, and the heart doth owe thee
More love, dead rose, than to any roses bold
Which Julia wears at dances, smiling cold: –
   Lie still upon this heart which breaks below thee!

A DENIAL

We have met late – it is too late to meet,
   O friend, not more than friend!
Death's forecome shroud is tangled round my feet,
And if I step or stir, I touch the end.
     In this last jeopardy
Can I approach thee, I, who cannot move?
How shall I answer thy request for love?
     Look in my face and see.

I love thee not, I dare not love thee! go
   In silence; drop my hand.
If thou seek roses, seek them where they blow
In garden-alleys, not in desert-sand.
     Can life and death agree,
That thou shouldst stoop thy song to my complaint?
I cannot love thee. If the word is faint,
     Look in my face and see.

I might have loved thee in some former days.
   Oh, then, my spirits had leapt
As now they sink, at hearing thy love-praise!
Before these faded cheeks were overwept,
     Had this been asked of me,
To love thee with my whole strong heart and head, –
I should have said still ... yes, but *smiled* and said,
     'Look in my face and see!'

But now ... God sees me, God, who took my heart
    And drowned it in life's surge.
In all your wide warm earth I have no part –
A light song overcomes me like a dirge.
        Could Love's great harmony
The saints keep step to when their bonds are loose,
Not weigh me down? am *I* a wife to choose?
        Look in my face and see –

While I behold, as plain as one who dreams,
    Some woman of full worth,
Whose voice, as cadenced as a silver stream's,
Shall prove the fountain-soul which sends it forth;
        One younger, more thought-free
And fair and gay, than I, thou must forget,
With brighter eyes than these ... which are not wet ...
        Look in my face and see!

So farewell thou, whom I have known too late
    To let thee come so near.
Be counted happy while men call thee great,
And one belovèd woman feels thee dear! –
        Not I! – that cannot be.
I am lost, I am changed, – I must go farther, where
The change shall take me worse, and no one dare
        Look in my face and see.

Meantime I bless thee. By these thoughts of mine
    I bless thee from all such!
I bless thy lamp to oil, thy cup to wine,
Thy hearth to joy, thy hand to an equal touch
        Of loyal troth. For me,
I love thee not, I love thee not! – away!
Here's no more courage in my soul to say
        'Look in my face and see.'

THE MEASURE: HYMN IV

He comprehended the dust of the earth in a measure
(שָׁלִישׁ). – *Isaiah* xl.
Thou givest them tears to drink in a measure
(שָׁלִישׁ). *Psalm* lxxx.

God the Creator, with a pulseless hand
Of unoriginated power, hath weighed
The dust of earth and tears of man in one
　　　Measure, and by one weight:
　　　So saith his holy book.

Shall we, then, who have issued from the dust
And there return, – shall we, who toil for dust,
And wrap our winnings in this dusty life,
　　　Say 'No more tears, Lord God!
　　　The measure runneth o'er'?

Oh, Holder of the balance, laughest Thou?
Nay, Lord! be gentler to our foolishness,
For his sake who assumed our dust and turns
　　　On Thee pathetic eyes
　　　Still moistened with our tears.

And teach us, O our Father, while we weep,
To look in patience upon earth and learn –
Waiting, in that meek gesture, till at last
These tearful eyes be filled
With the dry dust of death.

A CHILD'S THOUGHT OF GOD

They say that God lives very high;
   But if you look above the pines
You cannot see our God; and why?

And if you dig down in the mines
   You never see Him in the gold;
Though from Him all that's glory shines.

God is so good, He wears a fold
   Of heaven and earth across his face –
Like secrets kept, for love, untold.

But still I feel that his embrace
   Slides down by thrills, through all things made,
Through sight and sound of every place:

As if my tender mother laid
   On my shut lips her kisses' pressure,
Half-waking me at night, and said
   'Who kissed you through the dark, dear guesser?'

HECTOR IN THE GARDEN

Nine years old! The first of any
    Seem the happiest years that come:
    Yet when *I* was nine, I said
    No such word! I thought instead
That the Greeks had used as many
    In besieging Ilium.

Nine green years had scarcely brought me
    To my childhood's haunted spring;
    I had life, like flowers and bees.
    In betwixt the country trees,
And the sun the pleasure taught me
    Which he teacheth every thing.

If the rain fell, there was sorrow:
    Little head leant on the pane,
    Little finger drawing down it
    The long trailing drops upon it,
And the 'Rain, rain, come to-morrow,'
    Said for charm against the rain.

Such a charm was right Canidian,
    Though you meet it with a jeer!
    If I said it long enough,

Then the rain hummed dimly off,
And the thrush with his pure Lydian
   Was left only to the ear;

And the sun and I together
   Went a-rushing out of doors:
   We our tender spirits drew
   Over hill and dale in view,
Glimmering hither, glimmering thither
   In the footsteps of the showers.

Underneath the chestnuts dripping,
   Through the grasses wet and fair,
   Straight I sought my garden-ground
   With the laurel on the mound,
And the pear-tree oversweeping
   A side-shadow of green air.

In the garden lay supinely
   A huge giant wrought of spade!
   Arms and legs were stretched at length
   In a passive giant strength, –
The fine meadow turf, cut finely,
   Round them laid and interlaid.

Call him Hector, son of Priam!
    Such his title and degree.
    With my rake I smoothed his brow,
    Both his cheeks I weeded through,
But a rhymer such as I am,
    Scarce can sing his dignity.

Eyes of gentianellas azure,
    Staring, winking at the skies:
    Nose of gillyflowers and box;
    Scented grasses put for locks,
Which a little breeze at pleasure
    Set a-waving round his eyes:

Brazen helm of daffodillies,
    With a glitter toward the light;
    Purple violets for the mouth,
    Breathing perfumes west and south;
And a sword of flashing lilies,
    Holden ready for the fight:

And a breastplate made of daisies,
    Closely fitting, leaf on leaf;
    Periwinkles interlaced
    Drawn for belt about the waist;
While the brown bees, humming praises,
    Shot their arrows round the chief.

And who knows (I sometimes wondered)
    If the disembodied soul
    Of old Hector, once of Troy,
    Might not take a dreary joy
Here to enter – if it thundered,
    Rolling up the thunder-roll?

Rolling this way from Troy-ruin,
    In this body rude and rife
    Just to enter, and take rest
    'Neath the daisies of the breast –
They, with tender roots, renewing
    His heroic heart to life?

Who could know? I sometimes started
    At a motion or a sound!
    Did his mouth speak – naming Troy
    With an *ὀτοτοτοτοῖ*?
Did the pulse of the Strong-hearted
    Make the daisies tremble round?

It was hard to answer, often:
    But the birds sang in the tree,
    But the little birds sang bold
    In the pear-tree green and old,
And my terror seemed to soften
    Through the courage of their glee.

Oh, the birds, the tree, the ruddy
    And white blossoms sleek with rain!
    Oh, my garden rich with pansies!
    Oh, my childhood's bright romances!
All revive, like Hector's body,
    And I see them stir again.

And despite life's changes, chances,
    And despite the deathbell's toll,
    They press on me in full seeming.
    Help, some angel! stay this dreaming!
As the birds sang in the branches,
    Sing God's patience through my soul!

That no dreamer, no neglecter
    Of the present's work unsped,
    I may wake up and be doing,
    Life's heroic ends pursuing,
Though my past is dead as Hector,
    And though Hector is twice dead.

HIRAM POWERS'S GREEK SLAVE

They say Ideal Beauty cannot enter
The house of anguish. On the threshold stands
An alien Image with the shackled hands,
Called the Greek Slave: as if the artist meant her,
(That passionless perfection which he lent her,
Shadowed, not darkened, where the sill expands)
To, so, confront man's crimes in different lands,
With man's ideal sense. Pierce to the centre,
Art's fiery finger! – and break up ere long
The serfdom of this world! Appeal, fair stone,
From God's pure heights of beauty, against man's
        wrong!
Catch up in thy divine face, not alone
East griefs but west, – and strike and shame the
        strong,
By thunders of white silence, overthrown.

AMY'S CRUELTY

Fair Amy of the terraced house,
    Assist me to discover
Why you who would not hurt a mouse
    Can torture so your lover.

You give your coffee to the cat,
    You stroke the dog for coming,
And all your face grows kinder at
    The little brown bee's humming.

But when *he* haunts your door ... the town
    Marks coming and marks going ...
You seem to have stitched your eyelids down
    To that long piece of sewing!

You never give a look, not you,
    Nor drop him a 'Good morning,'
To keep his long day warm and blue,
    So fretted by your scorning.

She shook her head – 'The mouse and bee
    For crumb or flower will linger:
The dog is happy at my knee,
    The cat purrs at my finger.

'But *he* ... to *him*, the least thing given
    Means great things at a distance;

He wants my world, my sun, my heaven,
　　Soul, body, whole existence.

'They say love gives as well as takes;
　　But I'm a simple maiden, –
My mother's first smile when she wakes
　　I still have smiled and prayed in.

'I only know my mother's love
　　Which gives all and asks nothing;
And this new loving sets the groove
　　Too much the way of loathing.

'Unless he gives me all in change,
　　I forfeit all things by him:
The risk is terrible and strange –
　　I tremble, doubt, . . . deny him.

'He's sweetest friend or hardest foe,
　　Best angel or worst devil;
I either hate or . . . love him so,
　　I can't be merely civil!

'You trust a woman who puts forth
　　Her blossoms thick as summer's?
You think she dreams what love is worth,
　　Who casts it to new-comers?

'Such love's a cowslip-ball to fling,
    A moment's pretty pastime;
I give . . . all me, if anything,
    The first time and the last time.

'Dear neighbour of the trellised house,
    A man should murmur never,
Though treated worse than dog and mouse,
    Till doated on for ever!'

THE NORTH AND THE SOUTH
Rome, May, 1861
[Hans Christian Andersen visited Rome in 1861.]

'Now give us lands where the olives grow,'
    Cried the North to the South,
'Where the sun with a golden mouth can blow
Blue bubbles of grapes down a vineyard-row!'
    Cried the North to the South.

'Now give us men from the sunless plain,'
    Cried the South to the North,
'By need of work in the snow and the rain,
Made strong, and brave by familiar pain!'
    Cried the South to the North.

'Give lucider hills and intenser seas,'
    Said the North to the South.
'Since ever by symbols and bright degrees
Art, childlike, climbs to the dear Lord's knees,'
    Said the North to the South.

'Give strenuous souls for belief and prayer,'
    Said the South to the North,
'That stand in the dark on the lowest stair,
'While affirming of God, "He is certainly there,"'
    Said the South to the North.

'Yet oh for the skies that are softer and higher!'
    Sighed the North to the South;
'For the flowers that blaze, and the trees that aspire,
And the insects made of a song or a fire!'
    Sighed the North to the South.

'And oh for a seer to discern the same!'
    Sighed the South to the North;
'For a poet's tongue of baptismal flame,
To call the tree or the flower by its name!'
    Sighed the South to the North.

The North sent therefore a man of men
    As a grace to the South;
And thus to Rome came Andersen.
– *Alas, but must you take him again?*
        Said the South to the North.

FROM HEINE

I

Out of my own great woe
I make my little songs,
Which rustle their feathers in throngs
And beat on her heart even so.

They found the way, for their part,
Yet come again, and complain:
Complain, and are not fain
To say what they saw in her heart.

II

Art thou indeed so adverse?
Art thou so changed indeed?
Against the woman who wrongs me
I cry to the world in my need.

O recreant lips unthankful,
How could ye speak evil, say,
Of the man who so well has kissed you
On many a fortunate day?

III

My child, we were two children,
Small, merry by childhood's law;
We used to crawl to the hen-house
And hide ourselves in the straw.

We crowed like cocks, and whenever
The passers near us drew –
Cock-a-doodle! they thought
'Twas a real cock that crew.

The boxes about our courtyard
We carpeted to our mind,
And lived there both together –
Kept house in a noble kind.

The neighbour's old cat often
Came to pay us a visit;
We made her a bow and curtsey,
Each with a compliment in it.

After her health we asked
Our care and regard to evince –
(We have made the very same speeches
To many an old cat since).

We also sat and wisely
Discoursed, as old folk do,
Complaining how all went better
In those good times we knew, –

How love and truth and believing
Had left the world to itself,
And how so dear was the coffee,
And how so rare was the pelf.

The children's games are over,
The rest is over with youth –
The world, the good games, the good times,
The belief, and the love, and the truth.

IV

Thou lovest me not, thou lovest me not!
   'Tis scarcely worth a sigh:
Let me look in thy face, and no king in his place
   Is a gladder man than I.

Thou hatest me well, thou hatest me well –
   Thy little red mouth has told:
Let it reach me a kiss, and, however it is,
   My child, I am well consoled.

V

My own sweet Love, if thou in the grave,
   The darksome grave, wilt be,
Then will I go down by the side, and crave
   Love-room for thee and me.

I kiss and caress and press thee wild,
   Thou still, thou cold, thou white!
I wail, I tremble, and weeping mild,
   Turn to a corpse at the right.

The Dead stand up, the midnight calls,
   They dance in airy swarms –

We two keep still where the grave-shade falls,
    And I lie on in thine arms.

The Dead stand up, the Judgment-day
    Bids such to weal or woe –
But nought shall trouble us where we stay
    Embraced and embracing below.

VI

The years they come and go,
    The races drop in the grave,
Yet never the love doth so
    Which here in my heart I have.

Could I see thee but once, one day,
    And sink down so on my knee,
And die in thy sight while I say,
    'Lady, I love but thee!'

A MUSICAL INSTRUMENT

What was he doing, the great god Pan,
   Down in the reeds by the river?
Spreading ruin and scattering ban,
Splashing and paddling with hoofs of a goat,
And breaking the golden lilies afloat
   With the dragon-fly on the river.

He tore out a reed, the great god Pan,
   From the deep cool bed of the river:
The limpid water turbidly ran,
And the broken lilies a-dying lay,
And the dragon-fly had fled away,
   Ere he brought it out of the river.

High on the shore sat the great god Pan
   While turbidly flowed the river;
And hacked and hewed as a great god can,
With his hard bleak steel at the patient reed,
Till there was not a sign of the leaf indeed
   To prove it fresh from the river.

He cut it short, did the great god Pan,
   (How tall it stood in the river!)
Then drew the pith, like the heart of a man,

Steadily from the outside ring,
And notched the poor dry empty thing
    In holes, as he sat by the river.

'This is the way,' laughed the great god Pan
    (Laughed while he sat by the river),
'The only way, since gods began
To make sweet music, they could succeed.'
Then, dropping his mouth to a hole in the reed,
    He blew in power by the river.

Sweet, sweet, sweet, O Pan!
    Piercing sweet by the river!
Blinding sweet, O great god Pan!
The sun on the hill forgot to die,
And the lilies revived, and the dragon-fly
    Came back to dream on the river.

Yet half a beast is the great god Pan,
    To laugh as he sits by the river,
Making a poet out of a man:
The true gods sigh for the cost and pain, –
For the reed which grows nevermore again
    As a reed with the reeds in the river.

A VIEW ACROSS THE ROMAN CAMPAGNA
1861

Over the dumb Campagna-sea,
  Out in the offing through mist and rain,
Saint Peter's Church heaves silently
  Like a mighty ship in pain,
  Facing the tempest with struggle and strain.

Motionless waifs of ruined towers,
  Soundless breakers of desolate land:
The sullen surf of the mist devours
  That mountain-range upon either hand,
  Eaten away from its outline grand.

And over the dumb Campagna-sea
  Where the ship of the Church heaves on to wreck,
Alone and silent as God must be,
  The Christ walks. Ay, but Peter's neck
  Is stiff to turn on the foundering deck.

Peter, Peter! if such be thy name,
  Now leave the ship for another to steer,
And proving thy faith evermore the same,
  Come forth, tread out through the dark and drear,
  Since He who walks on the sea is here.

Peter, Peter! He does not speak;
　　He is not as rash as in old Galilee:
Safer a ship, though it toss and leak,
　　Than a reeling foot on a rolling sea!
　　And he's got to be round in the girth, thinks he.

Peter, Peter! He does not stir;
　　His nets are heavy with silver fish;
He reckons his gains, and is keen to infer
　　– 'The broil on the shore, if the Lord should wish;
　　But the sturgeon goes to the Cæsar's dish.'

Peter, Peter! thou fisher of men,
　　Fisher of fish wouldst thou live instead?
Haggling for pence with the other Ten,
　　Cheating the market at so much a head,
　　Griping the Bag of the traitor Dead?

At the triple crow of the Gallic cock
　　Thou weep'st not, thou, though thine eyes be dazed:
What bird comes next in the tempest-shock?
　　– Vultures! see, – as when Romulus gazed, –
　　To inaugurate Rome for a world amazed!

'DIED...'
(*The Times* Obituary)

What shall we add now? He is dead.
   And I who praise and you who blame,
   With wash of words across his name,
Find suddenly declared instead –
'*On Sunday, third of August, dead.*'

Which stops the whole we talked to-day.
   I, quickened to a plausive glance
   At his large general tolerance
By common people's narrow way,
Stopped short in praising. Dead, they say.

And you, who had just put in a sort
   Of cold deduction – 'rather, large
   Through weakness of the continent marge,
Than greatness of the thing contained' –
Broke off. Dead! – there, you stood restrained.

As if we had talked in following one
   Up some long gallery. 'Would you choose
   An air like that? The gait is loose –
Or noble.' Sudden in the sun
An oubliette winks. Where *is* he? Gone.

Dead. Man's 'I was' by God's 'I am' –
    All hero-worship comes to that.
    High heart, high thought, high fame, as flat
As a gravestone. Bring your *Jacet jam* –
The epitaph's an epigram.

Dead. There's an answer to arrest
    All carping. Dust's his natural place?
    He'll let the flies buzz round his face
And, though you slander, not protest?
– From such an one, exact the Best?

Opinions gold or brass are null.
    We chuck our flattery or abuse,
    Called Cæsar's due, as Charon's dues,
I' the teeth of some dead sage or fool,
To mend the grinning of a skull.

Be abstinent in praise and blame.
    The man's still mortal, who stands first,
    And mortal only, if last and worst.
Then slowly lift so frail a fame,
Or softly drop so poor a shame.

From AURORA LEIGH
FIRST BOOK

Of writing many books there is no end;
And I who have written much in prose and verse
For others' uses, will write now for mine, –
Will write my story for my better self,
As when you paint your portrait for a friend,
Who keeps it in a drawer and looks at it
Long after he has ceased to love you, just
To hold together what he was and is.

I, writing thus, am still what men call young;
I have not so far left the coasts of life
To travel inland, that I cannot hear
That murmur of the outer Infinite
Which unweaned babies smile at in their sleep
When wondered at for smiling; not so far,
But still I catch my mother at her post
Beside the nursery door, with finger up,
'Hush, hush – here's too much noise!' while her
    sweet eyes
Leap forward, taking part against her word
In the child's riot. Still I sit and feel
My father's slow hand, when she had left us both,
Stroke out my childish curls across his knee,
And hear Assunta's daily jest (she knew

He liked it better than a better jest)
Inquire how many golden scudi went
To make such ringlets. O my father's hand,
Stroke heavily, heavily the poor hair down,
Draw, press the child's head closer to thy knee!
I'm still too young, too young, to sit alone.
I write. My mother was a Florentine,
Whose rare blue eyes were shut from seeing me
When scarcely I was four years old, my life
A poor spark snatched up from a failing lamp
Which went out therefore. She was weak and frail;
She could not bear the joy of giving life,
The mother's rapture slew her. If her kiss
Had left a longer weight upon my lips
It might have steadied the uneasy breath,
And reconciled and fraternized my soul
With the new order. As it was, indeed,
I felt a mother-want about the world,
And still went seeking, like a bleating lamb
Left out at night in shutting up the fold, –
As restless as a nest-deserted bird
Grown chill through something being away,
        though what
It knows not. I, Aurora Leigh, was born
To make my father sadder and myself
Not overjoyous, truly. Women know
The way to rear up children (to be just),

They know a simple, merry, tender knack
Of tying sashes, fitting baby-shoes,
And stringing pretty words that make no sense,
And kissing full sense into empty words,
Which things are corals to cut life upon,
Although such trifles: children learn by such,
Love's holy earnest in a pretty play
And get not over-early solemnized,
But seeing, as in a rose-bush, Love's Divine
Which burns and hurts not, – not a single bloom, –
Become aware and unafraid of Love.
Such good do mothers. Fathers love as well
– Mine did, I know, – but still with heavier brains,
And wills more consciously responsible,
And not as wisely, since less foolishly;
So mothers have God's licence to be missed.

My father was an austere Englishman,
Who, after a dry lifetime spent at home
In college-learning, law, and parish talk,
Was flooded with a passion unaware,
His whole provisioned and complacent past
Drowned out from him that moment. As he stood
In Florence, where he had come to spend a month
And note the secret of Da Vinci's drains,
He musing somewhat absently perhaps
Some English question ... whether men should pay

The unpopular but necessary tax
With left or right hand – in the alien sun
In that great square of the Santissima
There drifted past him (scarcely marked enough
To move his comfortable island scorn)
A train of priestly banners, cross and psalm,
The white-veiled rose-crowned maidens holding up
Tall tapers, weighty for such wrists, aslant
To the blue luminous tremor of the air,
And letting drop the white wax as they went
To eat the bishop's wafer at the church;
From which long trail of chanting priests and girls,
A face flashed like a cymbal on his face
And shook with silent clangour brain and heart,
Transfiguring him to music. Thus, even thus,
He too received his sacramental gift
With eucharistic meanings; for he loved.

And thus beloved, she died. I've heard it said
That but to see him in the first surprise
Of widower and father, nursing me,
Unmothered little child of four years old,
His large man's hands afraid to touch my curls,
As if the gold would tarnish, – his grave lips
Contriving such a miserable smile
As if he knew needs must, or I should die,
And yet 't was hard, – would almost make the stones

Cry out for pity. There's a verse he set
In Santa Croce to her memory, –
'Weep for an infant too young to weep much
When death removed this mother' – stops the mirth
To-day on women's faces when they walk
With rosy children hanging on their gowns
Under the cloister to escape the sun
That scorches in the piazza. After which
He left our Florence and made haste to hide
Himself, his prattling child, and silent grief,
Among the mountains above Pelago;
Because unmothered babes, he thought, had need
Of mother nature more than others use,
And Pan's white goats, with udders warm and full
Of mystic contemplations, come to feed
Poor milkless lips of orphans like his own –
Such scholar-scraps he talked, I've heard from friends,
For even prosaic men who wear grief long
Will get to wear it as a hat aside
With a flower stuck in 't. Father, then, and child,
We lived among the mountains many years,
God's silence on the outside of the house,
And we who did not speak too loud within,
And old Assunta to make up the fire,
Crossing herself whene'er a sudden flame
Which lightened from the firewood, made alive
That picture of my mother on the wall.

*

The painter drew it after she was dead,
And when the face was finished, throat and hands,
Her cameriera carried him, in hate
Of the English-fashioned shroud, the last brocade
She dressed in at the Pitti; 'he should paint
No sadder thing than that,' she swore, 'to wrong
Her poor signora.' Therefore very strange
The effect was. I, a little child, would crouch
For hours upon the floor with knees drawn up,
And gaze across them, half in terror, half
In adoration, at the picture there, —
That swan-like supernatural white life
Just sailing upward from the red stiff silk
Which seemed to have no part in it nor power
To keep it from quite breaking out of bounds.
For hours I sat and stared. Assunta's awe
And my poor father's melancholy eyes
Still pointed that way. That way went my thoughts
When wandering beyond sight. And as I grew
In years, I mixed, confused, unconsciously,
Whatever I last read or heard or dreamed,
Abhorrent, admirable, beautiful,
Pathetical, or ghastly, or grotesque,
With still that face ... which did not therefore change,
But kept the mystic level of all forms,
Hates, fears, and admirations, was by turns
Ghost, fiend, and angel, fairy, witch, and sprite,

A dauntless Muse who eyes a dreadful Fate,
A loving Psyche who loses sight of Love,
A still Medusa with mild milky brows
All curdled and all clothed upon with snakes
Whose slime falls fast as sweat will; or anon
Our Lady of the Passion, stabbed with swords
Where the Babe sucked; or Lamia in her first
Moonlighted pallor, ere she shrunk and blinked
And shuddering wriggled down to the unclean;
Or my own mother, leaving her last smile
In her last kiss upon the baby-mouth
My father pushed down on the bed for that, –
Or my dead mother, without smile or kiss,
Buried at Florence. All which images,
Concentred on the picture, glassed themselves
Before my meditative childhood, as
The incoherencies of change and death
Are represented fully, mixed and merged,
In the smooth fair mystery of perpetual Life.
And while I stared away my childish wits
Upon my mother's picture (ah, poor child!),
My father, who through love had suddenly
Thrown off the old conventions, broken loose
From chin-bands of the soul, like Lazarus,
Yet had no time to learn to talk and walk
Or grow anew familiar with the sun, –
Who had reached to freedom, not to action, lived,

But lived as one entranced, with thoughts, not aims, –
Whom love had unmade from a common man,
But not completed to an uncommon man, –
My father taught me what he had learnt the best
Before he died and left me, – grief and love.
And, seeing we had books among the hills,
Strong words of counselling souls confederate
With vocal pines and waters, – out of books
He taught me all the ignorance of men,
And how God laughs in heaven when any man
Says 'Here I'm learned; this I understand;
In that, I am never caught at fault or doubt.'
He sent the schools to school, demonstrating
A fool will pass for such through one mistake,
While a philosopher will pass for such,
Through said mistakes being ventured in the gross
And heaped up to a system.
                                        I am like,
They tell me, my dear father. Broader brows
Howbeit, upon a slenderer undergrowth
Of delicate features, – paler, near as grave;
But then my mother's smile breaks up the whole,
And makes it better sometimes than itself.
So, nine full years, our days were hid with God
Among his mountains: I was just thirteen,
Still growing like the plants from unseen roots
In tongue-tied Springs, – and suddenly awoke

To full life and life's needs and agonies
With an intense, strong, struggling heart beside
A stone-dead father. Life, struck sharp on death,
Makes awful lightning. His last word was 'Love –'
'Love, my child, love, love!' – (then he had done
    with grief)
'Love, my child.' Ere I answered he was gone,
And none was left to love in all the world.

       *   *   *

I think I see my father's sister stand
Upon the hall-step of her country-house
To give me welcome. She stood straight and calm,
Her somewhat narrow forehead braided tight
As if for taming accidental thoughts
From possible pulses; brown hair pricked with grey
By frigid use of life (she was not old,
Although my father's elder by a year),
A nose drawn sharply, yet in delicate lines;
A close mild mouth, a little soured about
The ends, through speaking unrequited loves
Or peradventure niggardly half-truths;
Eyes of no colour, – once they might have smiled,
But never, never have forgot themselves
In smiling; cheeks, in which was yet a rose
Of perished summers, like a rose in a book,
Kept more for ruth than pleasure, – if past bloom,
Past fading also.

She had lived, we'll say,
A harmless life, she called a virtuous life,
A quiet life, which was not life at all
(But that, she had not lived enough to know),
Between the vicar and the county squires,
The lord-lieutenant looking down sometimes
From the empyrean to assure their souls
Against chance vulgarisms, and, in the abyss,
The apothecary, looked on once a year
To prove their soundness of humility.
The poor-club exercised her Christian gifts
Of knitting stockings, stitching petticoats,
Because we are of one flesh, after all,
And need one flannel (with a proper sense
Of difference in the quality) – and still
The book-club, guarded from your modern trick
Of shaking dangerous questions from the crease,
Preserved her intellectual. She had lived
A sort of cage-bird life, born in a cage,
Accounting that to leap from perch to perch
Was act and joy enough for any bird.
Dear heaven, how silly are the things that live
In thickets, and eat berries!
                                        I, alas,
A wild bird scarcely fledged, was brought to her cage,
And she was there to meet me. Very kind.
Bring the clean water, give out the fresh seed.

She stood upon the steps to welcome me,
Calm, in black garb. I clung about her neck, –
Young babes, who catch at every shred of wool
To draw the new light closer, catch and cling
Less blindly. In my ears my father's word
Hummed ignorantly, as the sea in shells,
'Love, love, my child.' She, black there with my grief,
Might feel my love – she was his sister once –
I clung to her. A moment she seemed moved,
Kissed me with cold lips, suffered me to cling,
And drew me feebly through the hall into
The room she sat in.

               There, with some strange spasm
Of pain and passion, she wrung loose my hands
Imperiously, and held me at arm's length,
And with two grey-steel naked-bladed eyes
Searched through my face, – ay, stabbed it through
    and through,
Through brows and cheeks and chin, as if to find
A wicked murderer in my innocent face,
If not here, there perhaps. Then, drawing breath,
She struggled for her ordinary calm –
And missed it rather, – told me not to shrink,
As if she had told me not to lie or swear, –
'She loved my father and would love me too
As long as I deserved it.' Very kind.

*

I understood her meaning afterward;
She thought to find my mother in my face,
And questioned it for that. For she, my aunt,
Had loved my father truly, as she could,
And hated, with the gall of gentle souls,
My Tuscan mother who had fooled away
A wise man from wise courses, a good man
From obvious duties, and, depriving her,
His sister, of the household precedence,
Had wronged his tenants, robbed his native land,
And made him mad, alike by life and death,
In love and sorrow. She had pored for years
What sort of woman could be suitable
To her sort of hate, to entertain it with,
And so, her very curiosity
Became hate too, and all the idealism
She ever used in life was used for hate,
Till hate, so nourished, did exceed at last
The love from which it grew, in strength and heat,
And wrinkled her smooth conscience with a sense
Of disputable virtue (say not, sin)
When Christian doctrine was enforced at church.

And thus my father's sister was to me
My mother's hater. From that day she did
Her duty to me (I appreciate it
In her own word as spoken to herself),

Her duty, in large measure, well pressed out,
But measured always. She was generous, bland,
More courteous than was tender, gave me still
The first place, – as if fearful that God's saints
Would look down suddenly and say 'Herein
You missed a point, I think, through lack of love.'
Alas, a mother never is afraid
Of speaking angerly to any child,
Since love, she knows, is justified of love.

And I, I was a good child on the whole,
A meek and manageable child. Why not?
I did not live, to have the faults of life:
There seemed more true life in my father's grave
Than in all England. Since *that* threw me off
Who fain would cleave (his latest will, they say,
Consigned me to his land), I only thought
Of lying quiet there where I was thrown
Like sea-weed on the rocks, and suffering her
To prick me to a pattern with her pin,
Fibre from fibre, delicate leaf from leaf,
And dry out from my drowned anatomy
The last sea-salt left in me.
                    So it was.
I broke the copious curls upon my head
In braids, because she liked smooth-ordered hair.
I left off saying my sweet Tuscan words

Which still at any stirring of the heart
Came up to float across the English phrase
As lilies (*Bene* or *Che che*), because
She liked my father's child to speak his tongue.
I learnt the collects and the catechism,
The creeds, from Athanasius back to Nice,
The Articles, the Tracts *against* the times
(By no means Buonaventure's 'Prick of Love'),
And various popular synopses of
Inhuman doctrines never taught by John,
Because she liked instructed piety.
I learnt my complement of classic French
(Kept pure of Balzac and neologism)
And German also, since she liked a range
Of liberal education, – tongues, not books.
I learnt a little algebra, a little
Of the mathematics, – brushed with extreme flounce
The circle of the sciences, because
She misliked women who are frivolous.
I learnt the royal genealogies
Of Oviedo, the internal laws
Of the Burmese empire, – by how many feet
Mount Chimborazo outsoars Teneriffe,
What navigable river joins itself
To Lara, and what census of the year five
Was taken at Klagenfurt, – because she liked
A general insight into useful facts.

I learnt much music, – such as would have been
As quite impossible in Johnson's day
As still it might be wished – fine sleights of hand
And unimagined fingering, shuffling off
The hearer's soul through hurricanes of notes
To a noisy Tophet; and I drew … costumes
From French engravings, nereids neatly draped
(With smirks of simmering godship): I washed in
Landscapes from nature (rather say, washed out).
I danced the polka and Cellarius,
Spun glass, stuffed birds, and modelled flowers in wax,
Because she liked accomplishments in girls.
I read a score of books on womanhood
To prove, if women do not think at all,
They may teach thinking (to a maiden aunt
Or else the author), – books that boldly assert
Their right of comprehending husband's talk
When not too deep, and even of answering
With pretty 'may it please you,' or 'so it is,' –
Their rapid insight and fine aptitude,
Particular worth and general missionariness,
As long as they keep quiet by the fire
And never say 'no' when the world says 'ay,'
For that is fatal, – their angelic reach
Of virtue, chiefly used to sit and darn,
And fatten household sinners, – their, in brief,
Potential faculty in everything

Of abdicating power in it: she owned
She liked a woman to be womanly,
And English women, she thanked God and sighed
(Some people always sigh in thanking God),
Were models to the universe. And last
I learnt cross-stitch, because she did not like
To see me wear the night with empty hands
A-doing nothing. So, my shepherdess
Was something after all (the pastoral saints
Be praised for't), leaning lovelorn with pink eyes
To match her shoes, when I mistook the silks;
Her head uncrushed by that round weight of hat
So strangely similar to the tortoise shell
Which slew the tragic poet.

                    By the way,
The works of women are symbolical.
We sew, sew, prick our fingers, dull our sight,
Producing what? A pair of slippers, sir,
To put on when you're weary – or a stool
To stumble over and vex you . . . 'curse that stool!'
Or else at best, a cushion, where you lean
And sleep, and dream of something we are not
But would be for your sake. Alas, alas!
This hurts most, this – that, after all, we are paid
The worth of our work, perhaps.

*   *   *

I had a little chamber in the house,
As green as any privet-hedge a bird
Might choose to build in, though the nest itself
Could show but dead-brown sticks and straws;
  the walls
Were green, the carpet was pure green, the straight
Small bed was curtained greenly, and the folds
Hung green about the window which let in
The out-door world with all its greenery.
You could not push your head out and escape
A dash of dawn-dew from the honeysuckle,
But so you were baptized into the grace
And privilege of seeing . . .
     First, the lime
(I had enough there, of the lime, be sure, –
My morning-dream was often hummed away
By the bees in it); past the lime, the lawn,
Which, after sweeping broadly round the house,
Went trickling through the shrubberies in a stream
Of tender turf, and wore and lost itself
Among the acacias, over which you saw
The irregular line of elms by the deep lane
Which stopped the grounds and dammed the overflow
Of arbutus and laurel. Out of sight
The lane was; sunk so deep, no foreign tramp
Nor drover of wild ponies out of Wales
Could guess if lady's hall or tenant's lodge

Dispensed such odours, – though his stick well-crooked
Might reach the lowest trail of blossoming briar
Which dipped upon the wall. Behind the elms,
And through their tops, you saw the folded hills
Striped up and down with hedges (burly oaks
Projecting from the line to show themselves),
Through which my cousin Romney's chimneys smoked
As still as when a silent mouth in frost
Breathes, showing where the woodlands hid
    Leigh Hall;
While, far above, a jut of table-land,
A promontory without water, stretched, –
You could not catch it if the days were thick,
Or took it for a cloud; but, otherwise,
The vigorous sun would catch it up at eve
And use it for an anvil till he had filled
The shelves of heaven with burning thunderbolts,
Protesting against night and darkness: – then,
When all his setting trouble was resolved
To a trance of passive glory, you might see
In apparition on the golden sky
(Alas, my Giotto's background!) the sheep run
Along the fine clear outline, small as mice
That run along a witch's scarlet thread.

Not a grand nature. Not my chestnut-woods
Of Vallombrosa, cleaving by the spurs

To the precipices. Not my headlong leaps
Of waters, that cry out for joy or fear
In leaping through the palpitating pines,
Like a white soul tossed out to eternity
With thrills of time upon it. Not indeed
My multitudinous mountains, sitting in
The magic circle, with the mutual touch
Electric, panting from their full deep hearts
Beneath the influent heavens, and waiting for
Communion and commission. Italy
Is one thing, England one.

                    On English ground
You understand the letter, – ere the fall
How Adam lived in a garden. All the fields
Are tied up fast with hedges, nosegay like;
The hills are crumpled plains, the plains parterres,
The trees, round, woolly, ready to be clipped,
And if you seek for any wilderness
You find, at best, a park. A nature tamed
And grown domestic like a barn-door fowl,
Which does not awe you with its claws and beak,
Nor tempt you to an eyrie too high up,
But which, in cackling, sets you thinking of
Your eggs to-morrow at breakfast, in the pause
Of finer meditation.

                  Rather say,
A sweet familiar nature, stealing in

173

As a dog might, or child, to touch your hand
Or pluck your gown, and humbly mind you so
Of presence and affection, excellent
For inner uses, from the things without.

*   *   *

SONNETS FROM THE PORTUGUESE

I thought once how Theocritus had sung
Of the sweet years, the dear and wished-for years,
To bear a gift for mortals, old or young:
And, as I mused it in his antique tongue,
I saw, in gradual vision through my tears,
The sweet, sad years, the melancholy years,
Those of my own life, who by turns had flung
A shadow across me. Straightway I was 'ware,
So weeping, how a mystic Shape did move
Behind me, and drew me backward by the hair:
And a voice said in mastery, while I strove, –
'Guess now who holds thee?' – 'Death,' I said.
       But, there,
The silver answer rang, – 'Not Death, but Love.'

*

But only three in all God's universe
Have heard this word thou hast said, – Himself, beside
Thee speaking, and me listening! and replied
One of us . . . *that* was God, . . . and laid the curse
So darkly on my eyelids, as to amerce
My sight from seeing thee, – that if I had died,
The deathweights, placed there, would have signified
Less absolute exclusion. 'Nay' is worse
From God than from all others, O my friend!
Men could not part us with their worldly jars,

175

Nor the seas change us, nor the tempests bend;
Our hands would touch for all the mountain-bars:
And, heaven being rolled between us at the end,
We should but vow the faster for the stars.

*

Unlike are we, unlike, O princely Heart!
Unlike our uses and our destinies.
Our ministering two angels look surprise
On one another, as they strike athwart
Their wings in passing. Thou, bethink thee, art
A guest for queens to social pageantries,
With gages from a hundred brighter eyes
Than tears even can make mine, to play thy part
Of chief musician. What hast *thou* to do
With looking from the lattice-lights at me,
A poor, tired, wandering singer, singing through
The dark, and leaning up a cypress tree?
The chrism is on thine head, – on mine, the dew, –
And Death must dig the level where these agree.

*

Thou hast thy calling to some palace-floor,
Most gracious singer of high poems! where
The dancers will break footing, from the care
Of watching up thy pregnant lips for more.
And dost thou lift this house's latch too poor
For hand of thine? and canst thou think and bear
To let thy music drop here unaware

In folds of golden fullness at my door?
Look up and see the casement broken in,
The bats and owlets builders in the roof!
My cricket chirps against thy mandolin.
Hush, call no echo up in further proof
Of desolation! there's a voice within
That weeps ... as thou must sing ... alone, aloof.

*

I lift my heavy heart up solemnly,
As once Electra her sepulchral urn,
And, looking in thine eyes, I overturn
The ashes at thy feet. Behold and see
What a great heap of grief lay hid in me,
And how the red wild sparkles dimly burn
Through the ashen greyness. If thy foot in scorn
Could tread them out to darkness utterly,
It might be well perhaps. But if instead
Thou wait beside me for the wind to blow
The grey dust up, ... those laurels on thine head,
O my Belovèd, will not shield thee so,
That none of all the fires shall scorch and shred
The hair beneath. Stand farther off then! go.

*

Go from me. Yet I feel that I shall stand
Henceforward in thy shadow. Nevermore
Alone upon the threshold of my door
Of individual life, I shall command

The uses of my soul, nor lift my hand
Serenely in the sunshine as before,
Without the sense of that which I forbore –
Thy touch upon the palm. The widest land
Doom takes to part us, leaves thy heart in mine
With pulses that beat double. What I do
And what I dream include thee, as the wine
Must taste of its own grapes. And when I sue
God for myself, He hears that name of thine,
And sees within my eyes the tears of two.

*

The face of all the world is changed, I think,
Since first I heard the footsteps of thy soul
Move still, oh, still, beside me, as they stole
Betwixt me and the dreadful outer brink
Of obvious death, where I, who thought to sink,
Was caught up into love, and taught the whole
Of life in a new rhythm. The cup of dole
God gave for baptism, I am fain to drink,
And praise its sweetness, Sweet, with thee anear.
The names of country, heaven, are changed away
For where thou art or shalt be, there or here;
And this ... this lute and song ... loved yesterday,
(The singing angels know) are only dear
Because thy name moves right in what they say.

What can I give thee back, O liberal
And princely giver, who hast brought the gold
And purple of thine heart, unstained, untold,
And laid them on the outside of the wall
For such as I to take or leave withal,
In unexpected largesse? am I cold,
Ungrateful, that for these most manifold
High gifts, I render nothing back at all?
Not so; not cold, – but very poor instead.
Ask God who knows. For frequent tears have run
The colours from my life, and left so dead
And pale a stuff, it were not fitly done
To give the same as pillow to thy head.
Go farther! let it serve to trample on.

*

Can it be right to give what I can give?
To let thee sit beneath the fall of tears
As salt as mine, and hear the sighing years
Re-sighing on my lips renunciative
Through those infrequent smiles which fail to live
For all thy adjurations? O my fears,
That this can scarce be right! We are not peers,
So to be lovers; and I own, and grieve,
That givers of such gifts as mine are, must
Be counted with the ungenerous. Out, alas!
I will not soil thy purple with my dust,
Nor breathe my poison on thy Venice-glass,

Nor give thee any love – which were unjust.
Beloved, I only love thee! let it pass.

*

Yet, love, mere love, is beautiful indeed
And worthy of acceptation. Fire is bright,
Let temple burn, or flax; an equal light
Leaps in the flame from cedar-plank or weed:
And love is fire. And when I say at need
I love thee . . . mark! . . . *I love thee* – in thy sight
I stand transfigured, glorified aright,
With conscience of the new rays that proceed
Out of my face toward thine. There's nothing low
In love, when love the lowest: meanest creatures
Who love God, God accepts while loving so.
And what I *feel*, across the inferior features
Of what I *am*, doth flash itself, and show
How that great work of Love enhances Nature's.

*

And therefore if to love can be desert,
I am not all unworthy. Cheeks as pale
As these you see, and trembling knees that fail
To bear the burden of a heavy heart, –
This weary minstrel-life that once was girt
To climb Aornus, and can scarce avail
To pipe now 'gainst the valley nightingale
A melancholy music, – why advert
To these things? O Belovèd, it is plain

I am not of thy worth nor for thy place!
And yet, because I love thee, I obtain
From that same love this vindicating grace,
To live on still in love, and yet in vain, –
To bless thee, yet renounce thee to thy face.

*

Indeed this very love which is my boast,
And which, when rising up from breast to brow,
Doth crown me with a ruby large enow
To draw men's eyes and prove the inner cost, –
This love even, all my worth, to the uttermost,
I should not love withal, unless that thou
Hadst set me an example, shown me how,
When first thine earnest eyes with mine were crossed,
And love called love. And thus, I cannot speak
Of love even, as a good thing of my own:
Thy soul hath snatched up mine all faint and weak,
And placed it by thee on a golden throne, –
And that I love (O soul, we must be meek!)
Is by thee only, whom I love alone.

*

And wilt thou have me fashion into speech
The love I bear thee, finding words enough,
And hold the torch out, while the winds are rough,
Between our faces, to cast light on each? –
I drop it at thy feet. I cannot teach
My hand to hold my spirit so far off

From myself – me – that I should bring thee proof
In words, of love hid in me out of reach.
Nay, let the silence of my womanhood
Commend my woman-love to thy belief, –
Seeing that I stand unwon, however wooed,
And rend the garment of my life, in brief,
By a most dauntless, voiceless fortitude,
Lest one touch of this heart convey its grief.

*

If thou must love me, let it be for nought
Except for love's sake only. Do not say
'I love her for her smile – her look – her way
Of speaking gently, – for a trick of thought
That falls in well with mine, and certes brought
A sense of pleasant ease on such a day' –
For these things in themselves, Belovèd, may
Be changed, or change for thee, – and love, so wrought,
May be unwrought so. Neither love me for
Thine own dear pity's wiping my cheeks dry, –
A creature might forget to weep, who bore
Thy comfort long, and lose thy love thereby!
But love me for love's sake, that evermore
Thou mayst love on, through love's eternity.

*

Accuse me not, beseech thee, that I wear
Too calm and sad a face in front of thine;
For we two look two ways, and cannot shine

With the same sunlight on our brow and hair.
On me thou lookest with no doubting care,
As on a bee shut in a crystalline;
Since sorrow hath shut me safe in love's divine,
And to spread wing and fly in the outer air
Were most impossible failure, if I strove
To fail so. But I look on thee – on thee –
Beholding, besides love, the end of love,
Hearing oblivion beyond memory;
As one who sits and gazes from above,
Over the rivers to the bitter sea.

*

And yet, because thou overcomest so,
Because thou art more noble and like a king,
Thou canst prevail against my fears and fling
Thy purple round me, till my heart shall grow
Too close against thine heart henceforth to know
How it shook when alone. Why, conquering
May prove as lordly and complete a thing
In lifting upward, as in crushing low!
And as a vanquished soldier yields his sword
To one who lifts him from the bloody earth,
Even so, Belovèd, I at last record,
Here ends my strife. If *thou* invite me forth,
I rise above abasement at the word.
Make thy love larger to enlarge my worth.

My poet, thou canst touch on all the notes
God set between his After and Before,
And strike up and strike off the general roar
Of the rushing worlds a melody that floats
In a serene air purely. Antidotes
Of medicated music, answering for
Mankind's forlornest uses, thou canst pour
From thence into their ears. God's will devotes
Thine to such ends, and mine to wait on thine.
How, Dearest, wilt thou have me for most use?
A hope, to sing by gladly? or a fine
Sad memory, with thy songs to interfuse?
A shade, in which to sing – of palm or pine?
A grave, on which to rest from singing? Choose.

*

I never gave a lock of hair away
To a man, Dearest, except this to thee,
Which now upon my fingers thoughtfully,
I ring out to the full brown length and say
'Take it.' My day of youth went yesterday;
My hair no longer bounds to my foot's glee,
Nor plant I it from rose or myrtle-tree,
As girls do, any more: it only may
Now shade on two pale cheeks the mark of tears,
Taught drooping from the head that hangs aside
Through sorrow's trick. I thought the funeral-shears
Would take this first, but Love is justified, –

Take it thou, – finding pure, from all those years,
The kiss my mother left here when she died.

*

The soul's Rialto hath its merchandise;
I barter curl for curl upon that mart,
And from my poet's forehead to my heart
Receive this lock which outweighs argosies, –
As purply black, as erst to Pindar's eyes
The dim purpureal tresses gloomed athwart
The nine white Muse-brows. For this counterpart, . . .
The bay-crown's shade, Belovèd, I surmise,
Still lingers on thy curl, it is so black!
Thus, with a fillet of smooth-kissing breath,
I tie the shadows safe from gliding back,
And lay the gift where nothing hindereth;
Here on my heart, as on thy brow, to lack
No natural heat till mine grows cold in death.

*

Belovèd, my Belovèd, when I think
That thou wast in the world a year ago,
What time I sat alone here in the snow
And saw no footprint, heard the silence sink
No moment at thy voice, but, link by link,
Went counting all my chains as if that so
They never could fall off at any blow
Struck by thy possible hand, – why, thus I drink
Of life's great cup of wonder! Wonderful,

185

Never to feel thee thrill the day or night
With personal act or speech, – nor ever cull
Some prescience of thee with the blossoms white
Thou sawest growing! Atheists are as dull,
Who cannot guess God's presence out of sight.

*

Say over again, and yet once over again,
That thou dost love me. Though the word repeated
Should seem 'a cuckoo-song,' as thou dost treat it,
Remember, never to the hill or plain,
Valley and wood, without her cuckoo-strain
Comes the fresh Spring in all her green completed.
Belovèd, I, amid the darkness greeted
By a doubtful spirit-voice, in that doubt's pain
Cry, 'Speak once more – thou lovest!' Who can fear
Too many stars, though each in heaven shall roll,
Too many flowers, though each shall crown the year?
Say thou dost love me, love me, love me – toll
The silver iterance! – only minding, Dear,
To love me also in silence with thy soul.

*

When our two souls stand up erect and strong,
Face to face, silent, drawing nigh and nigher,
Until the lengthening wings break into fire
At either curvèd point, – what bitter wrong
Can the earth do to us, that we should not long
Be here contented? Think. In mounting higher,

The angels would press on us and aspire
To drop some golden orb of perfect song
Into our deep, dear silence. Let us stay
Rather on earth, Belovèd – where the unfit
Contrarious moods of men recoil away
And isolate pure spirits, and permit
A place to stand and love in for a day,
With darkness and the death-hour rounding it.

*

Is it indeed so? If I lay here dead,
Wouldst thou miss any life in losing mine?
And would the sun for thee more coldly shine
Because of grave-damps falling round my head?
I marvelled, my Belovèd, when I read
Thy thought so in the letter. I am thine –
But . . . *so* much to thee? Can I pour thy wine
While my hands tremble? Then my soul, instead
Of dreams of death, resumes life's lower range.
Then, love me, Love! look on me – breathe on me!
As brighter ladies do not count it strange,
For love, to give up acres and degree,
I yield the grave for thy sake, and exchange
My near sweet view of Heaven, for earth with thee!

*

Let the world's sharpness, like a clasping knife,
Shut in upon itself and do no harm
In this close hand of Love, now soft and warm,

And let us hear no sound of human strife
After the click of the shutting. Life to life –
I lean upon thee, Dear, without alarm,
And feel as safe as guarded by a charm
Against the stab of worldlings, who if rife
Are weak to injure. Very whitely still
The lilies of our lives may reassure
Their blossoms from their roots, accessible
Alone to heavenly dews that drop not fewer,
Growing straight, out of man's reach, on the hill.
God only, who made us rich, can make us poor.

*

A heavy heart, Belovèd, have I borne
From year to year until I saw thy face,
And sorrow after sorrow took the place
Of all those natural joys as lightly worn
As the stringed pearls, each lifted in its turn
By a beating heart at dance-time. Hopes apace
Were changed to long despairs, till God's own grace
Could scarcely lift above the world forlorn
My heavy heart. Then *thou* didst bid me bring
And let it drop adown thy calmly great
Deep being! Fast it sinketh, as a thing
Which its own nature doth precipitate,
While thine doth close above it, mediating
Betwixt the stars and the unaccomplished fate.

I lived with visions for my company
Instead of men and women, years ago,
And found them gentle mates, nor thought to know
A sweeter music than they played to me.
But soon their trailing purple was not free
Of this world's dust, their lutes did silent grow,
And I myself grew faint and blind below
Their vanishing eyes. Then THOU didst come – to be,
Belovèd, what they seemed. Their shining fronts,
Their songs, their splendours (better, yet the same,
As river-water hallowed into fonts),
Met in thee, and from out thee overcame
My soul with satisfaction of all wants:
Because God's gifts put man's best dreams to shame.

*

My own Belovèd, who hast lifted me
From this drear flat of earth where I was thrown,
And, in betwixt the languid ringlets, blown
A life-breath, till the forehead hopefully
Shines out again, as all the angels see,
Before thy saving kiss! My own, my own,
Who camest to me when the world was gone,
And I who looked for only God, found *thee!*
I find thee; I am safe, and strong, and glad.
As one who stands in dewless asphodel
Looks backward on the tedious time he had
In the upper life, – so I, with bosom-swell,

Make witness, here, between the good and bad,
That Love, as strong as Death, retrieves as well.

*

My letters! all dead paper, mute and white!
And yet they seem alive and quivering
Against my tremulous hands which loose the string
And let them drop down on my knee to-night.
This said, – he wished to have me in his sight
Once, as a friend: this fixed a day in spring
To come and touch my hand . . . a simple thing,
Yet I wept for it! – this, . . . the paper's light . . .
Said, *Dear, I love thee*; and I sank and quailed
As if God's future thundered on my past.
This said, *I am thine* – and so its ink has paled
With lying at my heart that beat too fast.
And this . . . O Love, thy words have ill availed
If, what this said, I dared repeat at last!

*

I think of thee! – my thoughts do twine and bud
About thee, as wild vines, about a tree,
Put out broad leaves, and soon there's nought to see
Except the straggling green which hides the wood.
Yet, O my palm-tree, be it understood
I will not have my thoughts instead of thee
Who art dearer, better! Rather, instantly
Renew thy presence; as a strong tree should,
Rustle thy boughs and set thy trunk all bare,

190

And let these bands of greenery which insphere thee
Drop heavily down, – burst, shattered, everywhere!
Because, in this deep joy to see and hear thee
And breathe within thy shadow a new air,
I do not think of thee – I am too near thee.

*

I see thine image through my tears to-night
And yet to-day I saw thee smiling. How
Refer the cause? – Belovèd, is it thou
Or I, who makes me sad? The acolyte
Amid the chanted joy and thankful rite
May so fall flat, with pale insensate brow,
On the altar-stair. I hear thy voice and vow,
Perplexed, uncertain, since thou art out of sight,
As he, in his swooning ears, the choir's Amen.
Belovèd, dost thou love? or did I see all
The glory as I dreamed, and fainted when
Too vehement light dilated my ideal,
For my soul's eyes? Will that light come again,
As now these tears come – falling hot and real?

*

Thou comest! all is said without a word.
I sit beneath thy looks, as children do
In the noon-sun, with souls that tremble through
Their happy eyelids from an unaverred
Yet prodigal inward joy. Behold, I erred
In that last doubt! and yet I cannot rue

The sin most, but the occasion – that we two
Should for a moment stand unministered
By a mutual presence. Ah, keep near and close,
Thou dovelike help! and, when my fears would rise,
With thy broad heart serenely interpose:
Brood down with thy divine sufficiencies
These thoughts which tremble when bereft of those,
Like callow birds left desert to the skies.

*

The first time that the sun rose on thine oath
To love me, I looked forward to the moon
To slacken all those bonds which seemed too soon
And quickly tied to make a lasting troth.
Quick-loving hearts, I thought, may quickly loathe;
And, looking on myself, I seemed not one
For such man's love! – more like an out-of-tune
Worn viol, a good singer would be wroth
To spoil his song with, and which, snatched in haste,
Is laid down at the first ill-sounding note.
I did not wrong myself so, but I placed
A wrong on *thee*. For perfect strains may float
'Neath master-hands, from instruments defaced, –
And great souls, at one stroke, may do and doat.

*

Yes, call me by my pet-name! let me hear
The name I used to run at, when a child,
From innocent play, and leave the cowslips piled,

To glance up in some face that proved me dear
With the look of its eyes. I miss the clear
Fond voices which, being drawn and reconciled
Into the music of Heaven's undefiled,
Call me no longer. Silence on the bier,
While I call God – call God! – So let thy mouth
Be heir to those who are now exanimate.
Gather the north flowers to complete the south,
And catch the early love up in the late.
Yes, call me by that name, – and I, in truth,
With the same heart, will answer and not wait.

*

With the same heart, I said, I'll answer thee
As those, when thou shalt call me by my name –
Lo, the vain promise! is the same, the same,
Perplexed and ruffled by life's strategy?
When called before, I told how hastily
I dropped my flowers or brake off from a game,
To run and answer with the smile that came
At play last moment, and went on with me
Through my obedience. When I answer now,
I drop a grave thought, break from solitude;
Yet still my heart goes to thee – ponder how –
Not as to a single good, but all my good!
Lay thy hand on it, best one, and allow
That no child's foot could run fast as this blood.

If I leave all for thee, wilt thou exchange
And be all to me? Shall I never miss
Home-talk and blessing and the common kiss
That comes to each in turn, nor count it strange,
When I look up, to drop on a new range
Of walls and floors, another home than this?
Nay, wilt thou fill that place by me which is
Filled by dead eyes too tender to know change?
That's hardest. If to conquer love, has tried,
To conquer grief, tries more, as all things prove;
For grief indeed is love and grief beside.
Alas, I have grieved so I am hard to love.
Yet love me – wilt thou? Open thine heart wide,
And fold within the wet wings of thy dove.

*

When we met first and loved, I did not build
Upon the event with marble. Could it mean
To last, a love set pendulous between
Sorrow and sorrow? Nay, I rather thrilled,
Distrusting every light that seemed to gild
The onward path, and feared to overlean
A finger even. And, though I have grown serene
And strong since then, I think that God has willed
A still renewable fear ... O love, O troth ...
Lest these enclaspèd hands should never hold,
This mutual kiss drop down between us both
As an unowned thing, once the lips being cold.

And Love, be false! if *he*, to keep one oath,
Must lose one joy, by his life's star foretold.

*

Pardon, oh, pardon, that my soul should make,
Of all that strong divineness which I know
For thine and thee, an image only so
Formed of the sand, and fit to shift and break.
It is that distant years which did not take
Thy sovranty, recoiling with a blow,
Have forced my swimming brain to undergo
Their doubt and dread, and blindly to forsake
Thy purity of likeness and distort
Thy worthiest love to a worthless counterfeit:
As if a shipwrecked Pagan, safe in port,
His guardian sea-god to commemorate,
Should set a sculptured porpoise, gills a-snort
And vibrant tail, within the temple-gate.

*

First time he kissed me, he but only kissed
The fingers of this hand wherewith I write;
And ever since, it grew more clean and white,
Slow to world-greetings, quick with its 'Oh, list,'
When the angels speak. A ring of amethyst
I could not wear here, plainer to my sight,
Than that first kiss. The second passed in height
The first, and sought the forehead, and half missed,
Half falling on the hair. O beyond meed!

195

That was the chrism of love, which love's own crown,
With sanctifying sweetness, did precede.
The third upon my lips was folded down
In perfect, purple state; since when, indeed,
I have been proud and said, 'My love, my own.'

*

Because thou hast the power and own'st the grace
To look through and behind this mask of me
(Against which years have beat thus blanchingly
With their rains), and behold my soul's true face,
The dim and weary witness of life's race, –
Because thou hast the faith and love to see,
Through that same soul's distracting lethargy,
The patient angel waiting for a place
In the new Heavens, – because nor sin nor woe,
Nor God's infliction, nor death's neighbourhood,
Nor all which others viewing, turn to go,
Nor all which makes me tired of all, self-viewed, –
Nothing repels thee, . . . Dearest, teach me so
To pour out gratitude, as thou dost, good!

*

Oh, yes! they love through all this world of ours!
I will not gainsay love, called love forsooth.
I have heard love talked in my early youth,
And since, not so long back but that the flowers
Then gathered, smell still. Mussulmans and Giaours
Throw kerchiefs at a smile, and have no ruth

For any weeping. Polypheme's white tooth
Slips on the nut if, after frequent showers,
The shell is over-smooth, – and not so much
Will turn the thing called love, aside to hate
Or else to oblivion. But thou art not such
A lover, my Belovèd! thou canst wait
Through sorrow and sickness, to bring souls to touch,
And think it soon when others cry 'Too late.'

*

I thank all who have loved me in their hearts,
With thanks and love from mine. Deep thanks to all
Who paused a little near the prison-wall
To hear my music in its louder parts
Ere they went onward, each one to the mart's
Or temple's occupation, beyond call.
But thou, who, in my voice's sink and fall
When the sob took it, thy divinest Art's
Own instrument didst drop down at thy foot
To hearken what I said between my tears, . . .
Instruct me how to thank thee! Oh, to shoot
My soul's full meaning into future years,
That *they* should lend it utterance, and salute
Love that endures, from Life that disappears!

*

'*My future will not copy fair my past*' –
I wrote that once; and thinking at my side
My ministering life-angel justified

197

The word by his appealing look upcast
To the white throne of God, I turned at last,
And there, instead, saw thee, not unallied
To angels in thy soul! Then I, long tried
By natural ills, received the comfort fast,
While budding, at thy sight, my pilgrim's staff
Gave out green leaves with morning dews impearled.
I seek no copy now of life's first half:
Leave here the pages with long musing curled,
And write me new my future's epigraph,
New angel mine, unhoped for in the world!

*

How do I love thee? Let me count the ways.
I love thee to the depth and breadth and height
My soul can reach, when feeling out of sight
For the ends of Being and ideal Grace.
I love thee to the level of everyday's
Most quiet need, by sun and candle-light.
I love thee freely, as men strive for Right;
I love thee purely, as they turn from Praise.
I love thee with the passion put to use
In my old griefs, and with my childhood's faith.
I love thee with a love I seemed to lose
With my lost saints, – I love thee with the breath,
Smiles, tears, of all my life! – and, if God choose,
I shall but love thee better after death.

Belovèd, thou hast brought me many flowers
Plucked in the garden, all the summer through
And winter, and it seemed as if they grew
In this close room, nor missed the sun and showers.
So, in the like name of that love of ours,
Take back these thoughts which here unfolded too,
And which on warm and cold days I withdrew
From my heart's ground. Indeed, those beds and
    bowers
Be overgrown with bitter weeds and rue,
And wait thy weeding; yet here's eglantine,
Here's ivy! – take them, as I used to do
Thy flowers, and keep them where they shall not pine.
Instruct thine eyes to keep their colours true,
And tell thy soul their roots are left in mine.

THE BEST THING IN THE WORLD

What's the best thing in the world?
June-rose, by May-dew impearled;
Sweet south-wind, that means no rain;
Truth, not cruel to a friend;
Pleasure, not in haste to end;
Beauty, not self-decked and curled
Till its pride is over-plain;
Light, that never makes you wink;
Memory, that gives no pain;
Love, when, *so*, you're loved again.
What's the best thing in the world?
– Something out of it, I think.

LETTERS

R.B. TO E.B.B.

New Cross, Hatcham, Surrey.
January 10, 1845.

I love your verses with all my heart, dear Miss Barrett, –
and this is no off-hand complimentary letter that I shall
write, – whatever else, no prompt matter-of-course
recognition of your genius, and there a graceful and
natural end of the thing. Since the day last week when
I first read your poems, I quite laugh to remember how I
have been turning and turning again in my mind what
I should be able to tell you of their effect upon me, for
in the first flush of delight I thought I would this once
get out of my habit of purely passive enjoyment, when
I do really enjoy, and thoroughly justify my admira-
tion – perhaps even, as a loyal fellow-craftsman should,
try and find fault and do you some little good to be
proud of hereafter! – but nothing comes of it all – so
into me has it gone, and part of me has it become, this
great living poetry of yours, not a flower of which but
took root and grew – Oh, how different that is from
lying to be dried and pressed flat, and prized highly,
and put in a book with a proper account at top and
bottom, and shut up and put away ... and the book
called a 'Flora,' besides! After all, I need not give up the
thought of doing that, too, in time; because even now,

203

talking with whoever is worthy, I can give a reason for my faith in one and another excellence, the fresh strange music, the affluent language, the exquisite pathos and true new brave thought; but in this addressing myself to you – your own self, and for the first time, my feeling rises altogether. I do, as I say, love these books with all my heart – and I love you too. Do you know I was once not very far from seeing – really seeing you? Mr Kenyon said to me one morning 'Would you like to see Miss Barrett?' then he went to announce me, – then he returned … you were too unwell, and now it is years ago, and I feel as at some untoward passage in my travels, as if I had been close, so close, to some world's-wonder in chapel or crypt, only a screen to push and I might have entered but there was some slight, so it now seems, slight and just sufficient bar to admission, and the half-opened door shut, and I went home my thousands of miles, and the sight was never to be?

Well, these Poems were to be, and this true thankful joy and pride with which I feel myself,

Yours ever faithfully,
ROBERT BROWNING.

Miss Barrett
50 Wimpole Street.

E.B.B. TO R.B.

50 Wimpole Street: Jan. 11, 1845.

I thank you, dear Mr Browning, from the bottom of my heart. You meant to give me pleasure by your letter – and even if the object had not been answered, I ought still to thank you. But it is thoroughly answered. Such a letter from such a hand! Sympathy is dear – very dear to me: but the sympathy of a poet, and of such a poet, is the quintessence of sympathy to me! Will you take back my gratitude for it? – agreeing, too, that of all the commerce done in the world, from Tyre to Carthage, the exchange of sympathy for gratitude is the most princely thing!

For the rest you draw me on with your kindness. It is difficult to get rid of people when you once have given them too much pleasure – *that* is a fact, and we will not stop for the moral of it. What I was going to say – after a little natural hesitation – is, that if ever you emerge without inconvenient effort from your 'passive state,' and will *tell* me of such faults as rise to the surface and strike you as important in my poems, (for of course, I do not think of troubling you with criticism in detail) you will confer a lasting obligation on me, and one which I shall value so much, that I covet it at a distance. I do not pretend to any extraordinary meekness under criticism and it is possible enough that I might not be altogether obedient to yours. But with my high respect for your power in your Art and for your experience as an artist, it would be quite impossible for me to hear a general observation of yours on what appear to you my master-faults, without being the better for it hereafter in some way. I ask for only a sentence or two of general observation – and I do not ask even for *that*, so as to tease you – but in the humble, low voice, which is so excellent a thing in women – particularly when they go a-begging! The most frequent general criticism I receive, is, I think, upon the style, – 'if I *would* but change my style'! But *that* is an objection (isn't it?) to the writer bodily? Buffon says, and every sincere writer must feel, that *'Le style c'est l'homme'*; a fact, however, scarcely calculated to lessen the objection with certain critics.

Is it indeed true that I was so near to the pleasure and honour of making your acquaintance? and can it be true that you look back upon the lost opportunity with any regret? *But* – you know – if you had entered the 'crypt,' you might have caught cold, or been tired to death, and *wished* yourself 'a thousand miles off;' which would have been worse than travelling them. It is not my interest, however, to put such thoughts in your head about its being 'all for the best'; and I would rather hope (as I do) that what I lost by one chance I may recover by some future one. Winters shut me up as they do dormouse's eyes; in the spring, *we shall see:* and I am so much better that I seem turning round to the outward world again. And in the meantime I have learnt to know your voice, not merely from the poetry but from the kindness in it. Mr Kenyon often speaks of you – dear Mr Kenyon! – who most unspeakably, or only speakably with tears in my eyes, – has been my friend and helper, and my book's friend and helper! critic and sympathizer, true friend of all hours! You know him well enough, I think, to understand that I must be grateful to him.

I am writing too much, – and notwithstanding that I am writing too much, I will write of one thing more. I will say that I am your debtor, not only for this cordial letter and for all the pleasure which came with it, but in other ways, and those the highest: and I will say that while I live to follow this divine art of poetry, in proportion to my love for it and my devotion to it, I must be a devout admirer and student of your works. This is in my heart to say to you – and I say it.

And, for the rest, I am proud to remain

Your obliged and faithful
ELIZABETH B. BARRETT.

Robert Browning, Esq.,
New Cross, Hatcham, Surrey.

R.B. TO E.B.B.

Dear Miss Barrett, – I just shall say, in as few words as I can, that you make me very happy, and that, now the beginning is over, I dare say I shall do better, because my poor praise, number one, was nearly as felicitously brought out, as a certain tribute to no less a personage than Tasso, which I was amused with at Rome some weeks ago, in a neat pencilling on the plaister-wall by his tomb at Sant' Onofrio – 'Alla cara memoria – di – (please fancy solemn interspaces and grave capital letters at the new lines) di – Torquato Tasso – il Dottore Bernardini – offriva – il seguente Carme – O *tu'* – and no more, – the good man, it should seem, breaking down with the overload of love here! But my 'O tu' – was breathed out most sincerely, and now you have taken it in gracious part, the rest will come after. Only, – and which is why I write now – it looks as if I have introduced some phrase or other about 'your faults' so cleverly as to give exactly the opposite meaning to what I meant, which was, that in my first ardour I had thought to tell you of *everything* which impressed me in your verses, down, even, to whatever 'faults' I could find, – a good earnest, when I had got to *them*, that I had left out not much between – as if some Mr Fellows were to say, in the overflow of his first enthusiasm of rewarded adventure: 'I will describe you all the outer life and ways of these Lycians, down to their very sandal-thongs,' whereto the be-corresponded one rejoins – 'Shall I get next week, then, your dissertation on sandal-thongs?' Yes, and a little about the 'Olympian Horses,' and God-charioteers as well!

What 'struck me as faults,' were not matters on the removal of which, one was to have – poetry, or high poetry, – but the very highest poetry, so I thought, and that, to universal recognition. For myself, or any artist, in many of the cases there would be a positive loss of time, peculiar artist's pleasure – for an instructed eye loves to see where the brush has dipped twice in a lustrous colour, has lain insistingly along a favourite outline, dwelt lovingly in a grand shadow; for these 'too muches' for the everybody's picture are so many helps to the making out the real painter's picture as he had it in his brain. And all of the Titian's Naples Magdalen must have once been golden in its degree to justify that heap of hair in her hands – the *only* gold effected now!

But about this soon – for night is drawing on and I go out, yet cannot, quiet at conscience, till I report (to *myself*, for I never said it to you, I think) that your poetry must be, cannot but be, infinitely more to me than mine to you – for you *do* what I always wanted, hoped to do, and only seem now likely to do for the first time. You speak out, *you*, – I only make men and women speak – give you truth broken into prismatic hues, and fear the pure white light, even if it is in me, but I am going to try; so it will be no small comfort to have your company just now, seeing that when you have your men and women aforesaid, you are busied with them, whereas it seems bleak, melancholy work, this talking to the wind (for I have begun) – yet I don't think I shall let *you* hear, after all, the savage things about Popes and imaginative religions that I must say.

See how I go on and on to you, I who, whenever now and then pulled, by the head and hair, into letter-writing, get sorrowfully on for a line or two, as the cognate creature urged on by stick and string, and then come down 'flop' upon the sweet haven of page one, line last, as serene as the sleep of the virtuous! You will never more, I hope, talk of 'the honour of my acquaintance,' but I will joyfully wait for the delight of your friendship, and the spring, and my Chapel-sight after all!

Ever your most faithfully,
R. BROWNING.

For Mr Kenyon – I have a convenient theory about him, and his otherwise quite unaccountable kindness to me; but 'tis quite night now, and they call me.

E.B.B. TO R.B.

Dear Mr Browning, – The fault was clearly with me and not with you.

When I had an Italian master, years ago, he told me that there was an unpronounceable English word which absolutely expressed me, and which he would say in his own tongue, as he could not in mine – '*testa lunga.*' Of course, the signor meant *headlong!* – and now I have had enough to tame me, and might be expected to stand still in my stall. But you see I do not. Headlong I was at first, and headlong I continue – precipitously rushing forward through all manner of nettles and briars instead of keeping the path; guessing at the meaning of unknown words instead of looking into the dictionary – tearing open letters, and never untying a string, – and expecting everything to be done in a minute, and the thunder to be as quick as the lightning. And so, at your half word I flew at the whole one, with all its possible consequences, and wrote what you read. Our common friend, as I think he is, Mr Horne, is often forced to entreat me into patience and coolness of purpose, though his only intercourse with me has been by letter. And, by the way, you will be sorry to hear that during his stay in Germany *he* has been 'headlong' (out of a metaphor) twice; once, in falling from the Drachenfels, when he only just saved himself by catching at a vine; and once quite lately, at Christmas, in a fall on the ice of the Elbe in skating, when he dislocated his left shoulder in a very painful manner. He is doing quite well, I believe, but it was sad to have such a shadow from the German Christmas tree, and he a stranger.

In art, however, I understand that it does not do to be headlong, but patient and laborious – and there is a love strong enough, even in me, to overcome nature. I apprehend what you mean in the criticism you just intimate, and shall turn it over and over in my mind until I get practical good from it. What no mere critic sees, but what you, an artist, know, is the difference between the thing desired and the thing attained, between the idea in the writer's mind and the εἴδωλον cast off in his work. All the effort – the quick'ning of the breath and beating of the heart in pursuit, which is ruffling and injurious to the general effect of a composition; all which you call 'insistency,' and which many would call superfluity, and which is superfluous in a sense – you can pardon, because you understand. The great chasm between the thing I say, and the thing I would say, would be quite dispiriting to me, in spite even of such kindnesses as yours, if the desire did not master the despondency. 'Oh for a horse with wings!' It is wrong of me to write so of myself – only you put your finger on the root of a fault, which has, to my fancy, been a little misapprehended. I do not *say everything I think* (as has been said of me by master-critics) but I *take every means to say what I think*, which is different! – or I fancy so!

In one thing, however, you are wrong. Why should you deny the full measure of my delight and benefit from your writings? I could tell you why you should not. You have in your vision two worlds, or to use the language of the schools of the day, you are both subjective and objective in the habits of your mind. You can deal both with abstract thought and with human passion in the most passionate sense. Thus, you have an immense grasp in Art; and no one at all accustomed to consider the usual forms of it, could help regarding with reverence and gladness the gradual expansion of your powers. Then you are 'masculine' to the height – and I, as a woman, have studied some of your gestures of language and intonation wistfully, as a thing beyond me far! and the more admirable for being beyond.

E.B.B. TO R.B.

Feb. 3, 1845.

Why how could I hate to write to you, dear Mr
Browning? Could you believe in such a thing? If nobody
likes writing to everybody (except such professional
letter writers as you and I are *not*), yet everybody likes
writing to somebody, and it would be strange and
contradictory if I were not always delighted both to
hear from *you* and to write to *you*, this talking upon
paper being as good a social pleasure as another, when
our means are somewhat straitened. As for me, I have
done most of my talking by post of late years – as
people shut up in dungeons take up with scrawling
mottoes on the walls. Not that I write to many in the
way of regular correspondence, as our friend Mr Horne
predicates of me in his romances (which is mere roman-
cing!), but that there are a few who will write and be
written to by me without a sense of injury. Dear Miss
Mitford, for instance. You do not know her, I think,
personally, although she was the first to tell me (when
I was very ill and insensible to all the glories of the
world except poetry), of the grand scene in 'Pippa
Passes.' *She* has filled a large drawer in this room with
delightful letters, heart-warm and soul-warm, ... drift-
ings of nature (if sunshine could drift like snow), and

which, if they should ever fall the way of all writing, into print, would assume the folio shape as a matter of course, and take rank on the lowest shelf of libraries, with Benedictine editions of the Fathers, κ.τ.λ. I write this to you to show how I can have pleasure in letters, and never think them too long, nor too frequent, nor too illegible from being written in little 'pet hands.' I can read any MS. except the writing on the pyramids. And if you will only promise to treat me *en bon camarade*, without reference to the conventionalities of 'ladies and gentlemen,' taking no thought for your sentences (nor for mine), nor for your blots (nor for mine), nor for your blunt speaking (nor for mine), nor for your badd speling (nor for mine), and if you agree to send me a blotted thought whenever you are in the mind for it, and with as little ceremony and less legibility than you would think it necessary to employ towards your printer – why, *then*, I am ready to sign and seal the contract, and to rejoice in being 'articled' as your correspondent. Only *don't* let us have any constraint, any ceremony! *Don't* be civil to me when you feel rude, – nor loquacious when you incline to silence, – nor yielding in the manners when you are perverse in the mind. See how out of the world I am! Suffer me to profit by it in almost the only profitable circumstance, and let us rest from the bowing and the courtesying, you and I, on each side. You will find me an honest man on the whole, if rather hasty and prejudging, which is a different thing from prejudice at the worst. And we have great sympathies in common, and I am inclined to look up to you in many things, and to learn as much of everything as you will teach me. On the other hand you must prepare yourself to forbear and to forgive – will you? While I throw off the ceremony, I hold the faster to the kindness.

Is it true, as you say, that I 'know so "little" ' of you? And is it true, as others say, that the productions of an artist do not partake of his real nature, ... that in the minor sense, man is not made in the image of God? It is *not* true, to my mind – and therefore it is not true that I know little of you, except in as far as it is true (which I believe) that your greatest works are to come. Need I assure you that I shall always hear with the deepest interest every word you will say to me of what you are doing or about to do? I hear of the 'old room' and the ' "Bells" lying about,' with an interest which you may guess at, perhaps. And when you tell me besides, of *my poems being there*, and of your caring for them so much beyond the tidemark of my hopes, the pleasure rounds itself into a charm, and prevents its own expression. Overjoyed I am with this cordial sympathy – but it is better, I feel, to try to justify it by future work than to thank you for it now. I think – if I may dare to name myself with you in the poetic relation – that we both have high views of the Art we follow, and stedfast purpose in the pursuit of it, and that we should not, either of *us*, be likely to be thrown from the course, by the casting of any Atalanta-ball of speedy popularity. But I do not know, I cannot guess, whether you are liable to be pained deeply by hard criticism and cold neglect, such as original writers like yourself are too often exposed to – or whether the love of Art is enough for you, and the exercise of Art the filling joy of your life. Not that praise must not always, of necessity, be delightful to the artist, but that it may be redundant to his content. Do you think so? or not? It appears to me that poets who, like Keats, are highly susceptible to criticism, must be jealous, in their own persons, of the future honour of their works. Because, if a work is worthy, honour must follow it though the worker should not live to see that following overtaking. Now, is it not enough that the work be honoured – enough I mean, for the worker? And is it not enough to keep down a poet's ordinary wearing anxieties, to think, that if his work be worthy it will have honour, and, if not, that 'Sparta must have nobler sons than he'? I am writing nothing applicable, I see, to anything in question, but when one falls into a favourite train of thought, one indulges oneself in thinking on. I began in thinking and wondering what sort of artistic constitution you had, being determined, as you may observe (with a sarcastic smile at the impertinence), to set about knowing as much as possible of you immediately. Then you spoke of your 'gentle audience' (*you began*), and I, who know that you have not one but many enthusiastic admirers – the 'fit and few' in the intense meaning – yet not the *diffused* fame which will come to you presently, wrote on, down the margin of the subject, till I parted from it altogether. But, after all, we are on the proper matter of sympathy. And after all, and after all that has been said and mused upon the 'natural ills', the anxiety, and wearing out experienced by the true artist, – is not the *good* immeasurably greater than the *evil*? Is it not great good, and great joy? For my part, I wonder sometimes – I surprise myself wondering – how without such an object and purpose of life, people find it worth while to live at all. And, for happiness – why, my only idea of happiness, as far as my personal enjoyment is concerned, (but I have been straightened in some respects and in comparison with the majority of livers!) lies deep in poetry and its associations. And then, the escape from pangs of heart and bodily weakness – when you throw off *yourself* – what you feel to be *yourself* – into another atmosphere and into other relations, where your life may spread its wings out new, and gather on every separate plume a brightness from the sun of the sun! Is it possible that imaginative writers should be so fond of depreciating and lamenting over their own destiny?

Possible, certainly – but reasonable, not at all – and grateful, less than anything!

My faults, my faults – Shall I help you? Ah – you see them too well, I fear. And do you know that I also have something of your feeling about 'being about to *begin*,' or I should dare to praise you for having it. But in you, it is different – it is, in you, a virtue. When Prometheus had recounted a long list of sorrows to be endured by Io, and declared at last that he was μηδέπω ἐν προοιμίοις, poor Io burst out crying. And when the author of 'Paracelsus' and the 'Bells and Pomegranates' says that he is only 'going to begin' we may well (to take 'the opposite idea,' as you write) rejoice and clap our hands. Yet I believe that, whatever you may have done, you *will* do what is greater. It is my faith for you.

And how I should like to know what poets have been your sponsors, 'to promise and vow' for you, – and whether you have held true to early tastes, or leapt violently from them, and what books you read, and what hours you write in. How curious I could prove myself! – (if it isn't proved already).

But this is too much indeed, past all bearing, I suspect. Well, but if I ever write to you again – I mean, if you wish it – it may be in the other extreme of shortness. So do not take me for a born heroine of Richardson, or think that I sin always to this length, else, – you might indeed repent your quotation from Juliet – which I guessed at once – and of course –

> I have no joy in this contract to-day!
> It is too unadvised, too rash and sudden.

Ever faithfully yours,
ELIZABETH B. BARRETT.

E.B.B. TO R.B.

March 20, 1845.

Whenever I delay to write to you, dear Mr Browning, it is not, be sure, that I take my 'own good time,' but submit to my own bad time. It was kind of you to wish to know how I was, and not unkind of me to suspend my answer to your question – for indeed I have not been very well, nor have had much heart for saying so. This implacable weather! this east wind that seems to blow through the sun and moon! who can be well in such a wind? Yet for me, I should not grumble. There has been nothing very bad the matter with me, as there used to be – I only grow weaker than usual, and learn my lesson of being mortal, in a corner – and then all this must end! April is coming. There will be both a May and a June if we live to see such things, and perhaps, after all, we may. And as to seeing *you* besides, I observe that you distrust me, and that perhaps you penetrate my morbidity and guess how when the moment comes to see a living human face to which I am not accustomed, I shrink and grow pale in the spirit. Do you? You are learned in human nature, and you know the consequences of leading such a secluded life as mine – notwithstanding all my fine philosophy about social duties and the like – well – if you have such knowledge or if you have it not, I cannot say, but I do say that I will indeed see you when the warm weather has revived me a little, and put the earth 'to rights' again so as to make pleasures of the sort possible. For if you think that I shall not *like* to see you, you are wrong, for all your learning. But I shall be afraid of you at first – though I am not, in writing thus. You are Paracelsus, and I am a recluse, with nerves that have been all broken on the rack, and now hang loosely – quivering at a step and breath.

And what you say of society draws me on to many comparative thoughts of your life and mine. You seem to have drunken of the cup of life full, with the sun shining on it. I have lived only inwardly; or with *sorrow*, for a strong emotion. Before this seclusion of my illness, I was secluded still, and there are few of the youngest women in the world who have not seen more, heard more, known more, of society, than I, who am scarcely to be called young now. I grew up in the country – had no social opportunities, had my heart in books and poetry, and my experience in reveries. My sympathies drooped towards the ground like an untrained honey-suckle – and but for *one*, in my own house – but of this I cannot speak. It was a lonely life, growing green like the grass around it. Books and dreams were what I lived in – and domestic life only seemed to buzz gently around, like the bees about the grass. And so time passed, and passed – and afterwards, when my illness came and I seemed to stand at the edge of the world with all done, and no prospect (as appeared at one time) of ever passing the threshold of one room again; why then, I turned to thinking with some bitterness (after the greatest sorrow of my life had given me room and time to breathe) that I had stood blind in this temple I was about to leave – that I had seen no Human nature, that my brothers and sisters of the earth were *names* to me, that I had beheld no great mountain or river, noth-ing in fact. I was as a man dying who had not read Shakespeare, and it was too late! do you understand? And do you also know what a disadvantage this ignor-ance is to my art? Why if I live on and yet do not escape from this seclusion, do you not perceive that I labour under signal disadvantages – that I am, in a manner, as a *blind poet*? Certainly, there is a compensation to a degree. I have had much of the inner life, and from the habit of self-consciousness and self-analysis, I make great guesses at Human nature in the main. But how willingly I would as a poet exchange some of this lumbering, ponderous, helpless knowledge of books, for some experience of life and man, for some...

But all grumbling is a vile thing. We should all thank God for our measures of life, and think them enough for each of us. I write so, that you may not mistake what I wrote before in relation to society, although you do not see from my point of view; and that you may understand what I mean fully when I say, that I have lived all my chief *joys*, and indeed nearly all emotions that go warmly by that name and relate to myself personally, in poetry and in poetry alone. Like to write? Of course, of course I do. I seem to live while I write – it is life, for me. Why, what is to live? Not to eat and drink and breathe, – but to feel the life in you down all the fibres of being, passionately and joyfully. And thus, one lives in composition surely – not always – but when the wheel goes round and the procession is uninterrupted. Is it not so with you? oh – it must be so. For the rest, there will be necessarily a reaction; and, in my own particular case, whenever I see a poem of mine in print, or even smoothly transcribed, the reaction is most painful. The pleasure, the sense of power, without which I could not write a line, is gone in a moment; and nothing remains but disappointment and humiliation. I never wrote a poem which you could not persuade me to tear to pieces if you took me at the right moment! I have a *seasonable* humility, I do assure you.

Your friend in grateful regard,
E.B.B.

R.B. TO E.B.B.

May 24, 1845.

Don't you remember I told you, once on a time, that you 'knew nothing of me'? whereat you demurred – but I meant what I said, and knew it was so. To be grand in a simile, for every poor speck of a Vesuvius or a Stromboli in my microcosm there are huge layers of ice and pits of black cold water – and I make the most of my two of three fire-eyes, because I know by experience, alas, how these tend to extinction – and the ice grows and grows – still this last is true part of me, most characteristic part, *best* part perhaps, and I disown nothing – only, – when you talked of '*knowing* me'! Still, I am utterly unused, of these late years particularly, to dream of communicating anything about *that* to another person (all my writings are purely dramatic as I am always anxious to say) that when I make never so little an attempt, no wonder if I *bungle* notably – 'language,' too, is an organ that never studded this heavy heavy head of mine. Will you not think me very brutal if I tell you I could almost smile at your misapprehension of what I meant to write? – Yet I *will* tell you, because it will undo the bad effect of my thoughtlessness, and at the same time exemplify the point I have all along been honestly earnest to set you right upon ... my real inferiority to you; just that and no more. I wrote to you, in an unwise moment, on the spur of being again 'thanked,' and, unwisely writing just as if thinking to myself, said what must have looked absurd enough as seen apart from the horrible counterbalancing never-to-be-written *rest of me* – by the side of which, could it be written and put before you, my note would sink to its proper and relative place, and become a mere 'thank you' for your good opinion – which I assure you is far too generous – for I really believe you to be my superior in many respects, and feel uncomfortable till *you* see that, too – since I hope for your sympathy and assist-ance, and frankness is everything in such a case. I do assure you, that had you read my note, *only* having 'known' so much of me as is implied in having inspected, for instance, the contents, merely, of that fatal and often-referred-to 'portfolio' there (*Dii meliora piis!*), you would see in it, (the note not the portfolio) the blandest utterance ever mild gentleman gave birth to. But I forgot that one may make too much noise in a silent place by playing the few notes on the 'ear-piercing fife' which in Othello's regimental band might have been thumped into decent subordination by his 'spirit-stirring drum' – to say nothing of gong and ophicleide. Will you forgive me, on promise to remember for the future, and be more considerate? Not that you must too much despise me, neither; nor, of all things, apprehend I am attitudinizing à la Byron, and giving you to understand unutterable somethings, longings for Lethe and all that – far from it! I never committed murders, and sleep the soundest of sleeps – but 'the heart is desperately wicked,' that is true, and though I dare not say 'I know' mine, yet I have had signal opportunities, I who began life from the beginning, and can forget nothing (but names, and the date of the battle of Waterloo), and have known good and wicked men and women, gentle and simple, shaking hands with Edmund Kean and Father Mathew, you and – Ottima! Then, I had a certain faculty of self-consciousness, years and years ago, at which John Mill wondered, and which ought to be improved by this time, if constant use helps at all – and, meaning, on the whole, to be a Poet, if not *the* Poet . . . for I am vain and ambitious some nights, – I do myself justice, and dare call things by their names to myself, and say boldly, this I love, this I hate, this I would do, this I would not do, under all kinds of circumstances, –

and talking (thinking) in this style *to myself*, and beginning, however tremblingly, in spite of conviction, to write in this style *for myself* – on the top of the desk which contains my 'Songs of the Poets – NO.1 M.P.', I wrote, – what you now forgive, I know! Because I am, from my heart, sorry that by a foolish fit of inconsideration I should have given pain for a minute to you, towards whom, on every account, I would rather soften and 'sleeken every word as to a bird' ... (and, not such a bird as my black self that go screeching about the world for 'dead horse' – corvus (picus) – mirandola!) I, too, who have been at such pains to acquire the reputation I enjoy in the world, – (ask Mr Kenyon,) and who dine, and wine, and dance and enhance the company's pleasure till they make me ill and I keep house, as of late: Mr Kenyon, (for I only quote where you may verify if you please) *he* says my common sense strikes him, and its contrast with my muddy metaphysical poetry! And so it shall strike you – for though I am glad that, since you *did* misunderstand me, you said so, and have given me an opportunity of doing by another way what I wished to do in *that*, – yet, if you had *not* alluded to my writing, as I meant you should not, you would have certainly understood *something* of its drift when you found me next Tuesday precisely the same quiet (no, for I feel I speak too loudly, in spite of your kind disclaimer, but –) the same mild man-about-town you were gracious to, the other morning – for, indeed, my own way of worldly life is marked out long ago, as precisely as yours can be, and I am set going with a hand, winker-wise, on each side of my head, and a directing finger before my eyes, to say nothing of an instinctive dread I have that a certain whip-lash is vibrating somewhere in the neighbourhood in playful readiness! So 'I hope here be proofs,' Dogberry's satisfaction that, first, I am but a very poor creature compared to you and entitled by my wants to look up to you, – all I meant to say from the first of the first – and that, next, I shall be too much punished if, for this piece of mere inconsideration, you deprive me, more or less, or sooner or later, of the pleasure of seeing you, – a little over boisterous gratitude for which, perhaps, caused all the mischief! The reasons you give for deferring my visits next week are too cogent for me to dispute – that is too true – and, being now and henceforward 'on my good behaviour,' I will at once cheerfully submit to them, if needs must – but should your mere kindness and forethought, as I half suspect, have induced you to take such a step, you will now smile with me, at this new and very unnecessary addition to the 'fears of me' I have got so triumphantly over in your case! Wise man, was I not, to clench my first favourable impression so adroitly ... like a recent Cambridge worthy, my sister heard of; who, being on his theological (or rather, scripture-historical) examination, was asked by the Tutor, who wished to let him off easily, 'who was the first King of Israel?' – 'Saul' answered the trembling youth. 'Good!' nodded approvingly the Tutor. 'Otherwise called *Paul*,' subjoined the youth in his elation! Now I have begged pardon, and blushingly assured you *that* was only a slip of the tongue, and that I did really *mean* all the while, (Paul or no Paul), the veritable son of Kish, he that owned the asses, and found listening to the harp the best of all things for an evil spirit! Pray write me a line to say, 'Oh ... if *that's* all!' and remember me for good (which is very compatible with a moment's stupidity) and let me not for one fault, (and that the only one that shall be), lose *any pleasure* ... for your friendship I am sure I have not lost – God bless you, my dear friend!

R. BROWNING.

R.B. TO E.B.B.

September 25, 1845.

You have said to me more than once that you wished I might never know certain feelings *you* had been forced to endure. I suppose all of us have the proper place where a blow should fall to be felt most – and I truly wish *you* may never feel what I have to bear in looking on, quite powerless, and silent, while you are subjected to this treatment, which I refuse to characterize – so blind is it *for* blindness. I think I ought to understand what a father may exact, and a child should comply with; and I respect the most ambiguous of love's caprices if they give never so slight a clue to their all-justifying source. Did I, when you signified to me the probable objections – you remember what – to myself, my own happiness, – did I once allude to, much less argue against, or refuse to acknowledge those objections? For I wholly sympathize, however it go against me, with the highest, wariest, pride and love for you, and the proper jealousy and vigilance they entail – but now, and here, the jewel is not being over guarded, but ruined, cast away. And whoever is privileged to interfere should do so in the possessor's own interest – all common sense interferes – all rationality against absolute no-reason at all. And you ask whether you ought to obey this no-reason? I will tell you: all passive obedience and implicit submission of will and intellect is by far too easy, if well considered, to be the course prescribed by God to Man in this life of probation – for they *evade* probation altogether, though foolish people think otherwise. Chop off your legs, you will never go astray; stifle your reason altogether and you will find it is difficult to reason ill. 'It is hard to make these sacrifices!' – not so hard as to lose the reward or incur the penalty of an Eternity to come; 'hard to effect them, then, and go through with them' – *not* hard, when the leg is to be *cut off* – that it is rather harder to keep it quiet on a stool, I know very well. The partial indulgence, the proper exercise of one's faculties, there is the difficulty and problem for solution, set by that Providence which might have made the laws of Religion as indubitable as those of vitality, and revealed the articles of belief as certainly as that condition, for instance, by which we breathe so many times in a minute to support life. But there is no reward proposed for the feat of breathing, and a great one for that of believing – consequently there must go a great deal more of voluntary effort to this latter than is implied in the getting absolutely rid of it at once, by adopting the direction of an infallible church, or private judgment of another – for all our life is some form of religion, and all our action some belief, and there is but one law, however modified, for the greater and the less. In your case I do think you are called upon to do your duty to yourself; that is, to God in the end. Your own reason should examine the whole matter in dispute by every light which can be put in requisition; and every interest that appears to be affected by your conduct should have its utmost claims considered – your father's in the first place; and that interest, not in the miserable limits of a few days' pique or whim in which it would seem to express itself, but in its whole extent ... the *hereafter* which all momentary passion prevents him seeing ... indeed, the present on either side which everyone else must see. And this examination made, with whatever earnestness you will, I do think and am sure that on its conclusion you should act, in confidence that a duty has been performed ... *difficult*, or how were it a duty? Will it *not* be infinitely harder to act so than to blindly adopt his pleasure, and die under it? Who can *not* do that?

I fling these hasty rough words over the paper, fast as they will fall – knowing to whom I cast them, and that any sense they may contain or point to, will be caught and understood, and presented in a better light. The hard thing ... this is all I want to say ... is to act on one's own best conviction – not to abjure it and accept another will, and say '*there* is my plain duty' – easy it is, whether plain or no!

R.B. TO E.B.B.

January 28, 1846.

Ever dearest – I will say, as you desire, nothing on that subject – but this strictly for myself: you engaged me to consult my own good in the keeping or breaking our engagement; not *your* good as it might even seem to me; much less seem to another. My only good in this world – that against which all the world goes for nothing – is to spend my life with you, and be yours. You know that when I *claim* anything, it is really yourself in me – you *give* me a right and bid me use it, and I, in fact, am most obeying you when I appear most exacting on my own account – so, in that feeling, I dare claim, once for all, and in all possible cases (except that dreadful one of your becoming worse again ... in which case I wait till life ends with both of us), I claim your promise's fulfilment – say, at the summer's end: it cannot be for your good that this state of things should continue. We can go to Italy for a year or two and be happy as day and night are long. For me, I adore you. This is all unnecessary, I feel as I write: but you will think of the main fact as *ordained*, granted by God, will you not, dearest? – so, not to be put in doubt *ever again* – then, we can go quietly thinking of after matters. Till tomorrow, and ever after, God bless my heart's own, own Ba. All my soul follows you, love – encircles you – and I live in being yours.

E.B.B. TO R.B.

Let it be this way, ever dearest. If in the time of fine weather, I am not ill, ... *then* ... *not now* ... you shall decide, and your decision shall be duty and desire to me, both – I will make no difficulties. Remember, in the meanwhile, that I *have* decided to let it be as you shall choose ... *shall* choose. That I love you enough to give you up 'for your good,' is proof (to myself at least) that I love you enough for any other end: – but you thought *too much of me in the last letter*. Do not mistake me. I believe and trust in all your words – only you are generous unawares, as other men are selfish.

More, I meant to say of this; but you moved me as usual yesterday into the sunshine, and then I am dazzled and cannot see clearly. Still I see that you love me and that I am bound to you! – and 'what more need I see,' you may ask; while I cannot help looking out to the future, to the blue ridges of the hills, to the *chances* of your being happy with me. Well! I am yours as *you* see ... and not yours to teaze you. You shall decide everything when the time comes for doing anything ... and from this to then, I do not, dearest, expect you to use 'the liberty of leaping out of the window,' unless you are sure of the house being on fire! Nobody shall push you out of the window – least of all, *I*.

For Italy ... you are right. We should be nearer the sun, as you say, and further from the world, as I think – out of hearing of the great storm of gossiping, when 'scirocco is loose.' Even if you liked to live altogether abroad, coming to England at intervals, it would be no sacrifice for me – and whether in Italy or England, we should have sufficient or more than sufficient means of living, without modifying by a line that 'good free life' of yours which you reasonably praise – which, if it had been necessary to modify, *we must have parted*, ... because I could not have borne to see you do it; though, that you once offered it for my sake, I never shall forget. ✳✳✳

✳✳✳

E.B.B. TO R.B.

March 4, 1846.

✳✳✳ You do not see aright what I meant to tell you on another subject. If he was displeased, (and it was expressed by a shadow a mere negation of pleasure) it was not with you as a visitor and my friend. You must not fancy such a thing. It was a sort of instinctive indisposition towards seeing you here – unexplained to himself, I have no doubt – of course unexplained, or he would have desired me to receive you never again, *that* would have been done at once and unscrupulously. But without defining his own feeling, he rather disliked seeing you here – it just touched one of his vibratory wires, brushed by and touched it – oh, we understand in this house. He is not a nice observer, but, at intervals very wide, he is subject to lightnings – call them fancies, sometimes right, sometimes wrong. Certainly it was not in the character of a 'sympathizing friend' that you made him a very little cross on Monday. And yet you never were nor will be in danger of being *thanked*, he would not think of it. For the reserve, the apprehension – dreadful those things are, and desecrating to one's own nature – but we did not make this position, we only endure it. The root of the evil is the miserable misconception of the limits and character of parental rights – it is a mistake of the intellect rather than of the heart. Then, after using one's children as one's chattels for a time, the children drop lower and lower toward the level of the chattels, and the duties of human sympathy to them become difficult in proportion. And (it seems strange to say it, yet it is true) *love*, he does not conceive of at all. He has feeling, he can be moved deeply, he is capable of affection in a peculiar way, but *that*, he does not understand, any more than he understands Chaldee, respecting it less of course.

And you fancy that I could propose Italy again? after saying too that I never would? Oh no, no – yet there is time to think of this, a superfluity of time, ... 'time, times and half a time' and to make one's head swim with leaning over a precipice is not wise. The roar of the world comes up too, as you hear and as I heard from the beginning. There will be no lack of 'lying,' be sure – 'pure lying' too – and nothing you can do, dearest dearest, shall hinder my being torn to pieces by most of the particularly affectionate friends I have in the world. Which I do not think of much, any more than of Italy. You will be mad, and I shall be bad ... and *that* will be the effect of being poets! 'Till when, where are you?' – why in the very deepest of my soul – wherever in it is the fountain head of loving! beloved, *there* you are!

Some day I shall ask you 'in form,' – as I care so much for forms, it seems, – what your 'faults' are, these immense multitudinous faults of yours, which I hear such talk of, and never, never can get to see. Will you give me a catalogue raisonnée of your faults? I should like it, I think. In the meantime they seem to be faults of obscurity, that is, invisible faults, like those in the poetry which do not keep it from selling as I am *so, so* glad to understand. I am glad too that Mr Milnes knows you a little.

Now I must end, there is no more time to-night. God bless you, very dearest! Keep better ... try to be well –

as *I* do for you since you ask me. Did I ever think that *you* would think it worth while to ask me *that*? What a dream! reaching out into the morning! To-day however I did not go down-stairs, because it was colder and the wind blew its way into the passages: if I can to-morrow without risk, I will, . . . be sure . . . be sure. Till Thursday then! – till eternity!

'Till when, where am I,' but with you? and what, but yours

Your
BA.

E.B.B. TO R.B.

May 26, 1846.

My beloved I scarcely know what to say about the poem. It is almost profane and a sin to keep you from writing it when your mind goes that way, – yet I am afraid that you cannot begin without doing too much and without suffering as a consequence in your head. Now if you make yourself ill, what will be the end? So you see my fears! Let it be however as it must be! Only you will promise to keep from all excesses, and to write very very gently. Ah – can you keep such a promise, if it is made ever so? There are the fears again.

You are very strange in what you say about my reading your poetry – as if it were not my peculiar gladness and glory! – my own, which no man can take from me. And not *you*, indeed! Yet I am not likely to mistake your poetry for the flower of your nature, knowing what that flower is, knowing something of what that flower is without a name, and feeling something of the mystical perfume of it. When I said, or when others said for me, that my poetry was the flower of me, was it praise, did you think, or blame? might it not stand for a sarcasm? It might, – if it were not true, miserably true after a fashion.

Yet something of the sort is true, of course, with all poets who write directly from their personal experience and emotions – their ideal rises to the surface and floats like the bell of the waterlily. The roots and the muddy water are *sub-audita*, you know – as surely there, as the flower.

But *you* … you have the superabundant mental life and individuality which admits of shifting a personality and speaking the truth still. *That* is the highest faculty, the strongest and rarest, which exercises itself in Art, – we are all agreed there is none so great faculty as the dramatic. Several times you have hinted to me that I made you careless for the drama, and it has puzzled me to fancy how it could be, when I understand myself so clearly both the difficulty and the glory of dramatic art. Yet I am conscious of wishing you to take the other crown besides – and after having made your own creatures speak in clear human voices, to speak yourself out of that personality which God made, and with the voice which He tuned into such power and sweetness of speech. I do not think that, with all that music in you, only your own personality should be dumb, nor that having thought so much and deeply on life and its ends, you should not teach what you have learnt, in the directest and most impressive way, the mask thrown off however moist with the breath. And it is not, I believe, by the dramatic medium, that poets teach most impressively – I have seemed to observe *that*! ... it is too difficult for the common reader to analyse, and to discern between the vivid and the earnest. Also he is apt to understand better always, when he sees the lips move. Now, here is yourself, with your wonderful faculty! – it is wondered at and recognized on all sides where there are eyes to see – it is called wonderful and admirable! Yet, with an inferior power, you might have taken yourself closer to the hearts and lives of men, and made yourself dearer, though being less great. Therefore I do want you to do this with your surpassing power – it will be so easy to you to speak, and so noble, when spoken.

Not that I usen't to fancy I could see you and know you, in a reflex image, in your creations! I used, you remember. How these broken lights and forms look strange and unlike now to me, when I stand by the complete idea. Yes, *now* I feel that no one can know you worthily by those poems. Only ... I guessed a little. *Now* let us have your own voice speaking of yourself – if the voice may not hurt the speaker – which is my fear. ***

***

R.B. to his sister.

June 1861.

Dearest, I know I have shocked you deeply, and perhaps more than was needed, but you must forgive me and consider the need of doing something at once, as the news might have reached you even more abruptly, – and my own stupid state of mind yesterday. I can't even yet say of myself whether I was surprised or not, by this calamity; there is such a balance of reasons for fear (reasons for reassurance as they seemed then) that I don't know what I feel nor felt. She had been gravely affected by a series of misfortunes moral and physical – or united, as they always were. The Villafranca Peace and the illness with it thro' the summer at Siena the year before last, last year's still worse trial for six months together, the daily waiting for news from Henrietta and the end (stopping as it did all chance of good and reparation from the summer) rendered her weaker – weaker – she did *nothing* at Rome, took some three or four little drives, never walked two paces out of the room, so could not but be in a worse state to meet an illness: yet, on the other hand, her cheerfulness, and the quick succeeding of good and quiet looks to the suffering, and the quiet of the last six months, made everyone say 'how wonderfully she recovers, – she will soon be strong again, another *quiet* summer and *then*,' &c. &c. Also her own impressions were in furtherance of this hope, and when I determined to forego the journey to Paris, in opposition to her expressed wishes, I not only knew but got her to confess candidly that for *herself* the reprieve from going and the trials it would entail on her would be an inestimable advantage – only, 'still,' 'for my sake,' &c., she would run the risk. I would not, however. We travelled, as I have told you, easily and with as little fatigue as possible, and on reaching here I let her repose at will, not asking her to go out, but take the air and exercise of the large rooms to begin with. She saw no one, two or three friends at most, had no one to tea (except when intimates looked in once or twice) and began to look well, everybody said. But the weather was suffocatingly hot, and she said to me 'My cough has got well at once, as is always the way in such weather, but, curiously, it begins to affect me, as usual.' I said 'Let us *go* at once.' We talked of places, the choice being with respect to her different requirements – when last Thursday week it seems that, while I was away at the newsroom, Miss Blagden came, say at six or seven in the evening: the windows which had been closely shut all day (as the only way of excluding the burning external air) were opened to the ground to admit the breeze which usually springs up after such days, and she placed her chair, I am told, in the doorway, between cross draughts of many windows – all the rooms opening into each other, – whereupon Isa B. remonstrated, but Ba said 'Oh, the cushion at the back of the chair prevents my suffering.' It was her constant way, besides. I came in and we had tea, and then she remarked 'I think I have a sore throat.'

Next day was past just as usual, only she told me she had a cold: at night she coughed much and sate up, restlessly, a good deal, and next morning took two Cooper's pills, I afterwards heard, with a view to staving off the attack she felt imminent: still, nothing happened unusual in the day, but toward night she felt so oppressed that she said, 'I think you shall go and get me a blister and a little Ipecacuanha wine, to relieve the oppression: I find the medicine has acted inordinately,' –

she rarely had recourse to it, but had taken this dose before with benefit – this time, the effects were beyond her expectation. I ran (at 10 p.m.) to the chemist's, got and applied the blister, and administered the wine but she seemed little relieved till at 1 o'clock about or later she began to suffer distressingly from the accumulation of phlegm, which she had no power to cough up. I left her with Annunziata, dressed and knocked up (with difficulty) Dr Wilson, a physician of great repute here, and specially conversant in maladies of the chest: he followed with me, and we found her worse, labouring most distressingly and ineffectually: Wilson prescribed promptly – got two prescriptions made up by two chymists (our porter and I got them), put on sinapisms to breast and back, and hot water with mustard to the feet. For a long while she continued unrelieved – he remained till nearly *five*. At last she recovered and we hoped all was over, but this was the second night she had passed in violent exertion without a minute's sleep. From this time things went on thus, – the symptoms were said to be always 'a little better'; but Wilson examined carefully and reported, with a very serious face, that one lung was condensed (the right) and that he suspected an abscess in it; but he was aware of her long previous experience of the possibility of making shift with damaged lungs, and could not say how it might be – 'it would require a long time to get well.' I told part of this to Ba who repeatedly answered 'it is the old story – they don't know my case – I have been tapped and sounded so, and condemned so, repeatedly: this time it is said the right is the affected lung while the left is free – Dr Chambers said just the contrary. This is only one of my old attacks. I know all about it and I shall get better' – 'It was not so bad an attack as that of two years ago,' and so she continued: every day I carried her into the drawing-room where she sate only in her nightgown in her own chair, for the airiness of the room. She read newspapers, a little – saw nobody of course – going to bed about seven; I sate up most nights, – lay down by her only once, I think, or twice at most, when I was up so often that I discontinued it, which she seemed not to notice; for we brought a small bed into the drawing-room and placed her in it, and she began to doze very much, restlessly, and seemed unaware I was not in bed on a sopha behind: from the first the prescription was 'nourishment, even wine, a little, often if in small quantities.' But Ba never could or would try to take solid nourishment: she had strong brodo (clear soup) but would take nothing else.

So we went on, 'rather better, but still with the unfavourable symptoms' – was I told twice a day. She was cheerful as ever, with voice all but extinct – still, 'it would be nothing' she repeated. On Thursday night we tried asses' milk, with success – 'had a better night decidedly' – always much expectoration however, and her feet swelled a little. I let Isa Blagden come and kiss her: she whispered 'I am decidedly better,' and gave that impression to Isa. On Friday she had asses' milk, broth twice, some bread and butter: we talked about our plans – about the house, Casa Guidi, which had suddenly grown distasteful to both of us, noisy, hot, close – poor place we have liked so for fourteen years! I said 'it would be best to take a Villa – you decide on Rome for the winter, and properly, – what good of coming in the summer to a town house you cannot stay in?' She said 'Ah, but I can't leave Florence, I like Florence, – you would like to establish ourselves in Rome.' I said 'no, there's Villa Niccolini, for instance – that would just suit.' She said 'that would suit – try, inquire' – and after seemed so interested about it that I said 'There's no hurry, – we can get in there at once if you like, and it will be just as cool as Siena, with the convenience of being near the city.' 'Oh,' she said, 'that's not it – we must change the air now, that is my one chance. I meant, that if you take it for three years you can send up our furniture and we can enter at once in it when we return next spring.' I observed a tendency to light headedness in all this – as she did – complaining of it to the doctor, and telling me how she had strange thoughts, about the windows, which 'seemed to be hung in the Hungarian colours.' And she smiled to Isa Blagden, at eight on

Friday, as she took the glass, 'Oh, I not only have asses' milk but asses' thoughts – I am so troubled with silly politics and nonsense.' Isa told her something she had heard about the politics of Ricasoli which interested her so much that I interposed – 'No talking, come, go Isa' – and I pushed her out; but Isa says that while my back was turned for a moment to pour out some medicine she whispered 'Did you say Ricasoli said his politics were identical with those of Cavour, only they took different views of the best way of carrying them out?' – Yes – 'Ah, so I thought.' Isa left convinced she was better, the doctor came – 'perhaps a little better.' We talked over her aversion to food. I caused to be made a very strong fowl-jelly, placed in ice in readiness, and then asked if she would not try it during the night – 'no'. I did not know how little good it would do – the weakness came from other causes, and *these* were important, the other could be easily got rid of. I sat by her at night. She coughed little, took the emulgent duly, and another medicine, but dozed constantly: if I spoke she looked, knew me, smiled, said she was better, and relapsed. I continued this till past three in the morning, when the dozing made me very uneasy. She said 'You did right not to wait – what a fine steamer – how comfortable!' I called Annunziata, bade her get hot water, as the Doctor had done, and send the porter for himself. I bade her sit up for the water. She did with little help –

smiling, letting us act, and repeating 'Well, you do make an exaggerated case of it!' 'My hands too' she said and put them in another basin. I said you know me? 'My Robert – my heavens, my beloved' – kissing me (but I can't tell you) she said 'Our lives are held by God.' I asked, 'will you take jelly for my sake?' 'Yes.' I brought a saucerful and fed it by spoonfuls into her mouth. I then brought a second, and poured some into a glass – she took all. She put her arms round me – 'God bless you' repeatedly – kissing me with such vehemence that when I laid her down she continued to kiss the air with her lips, and several times raised her own hands and kissed them; I said 'Are you comfortable?' 'Beautiful.' I only put in a thing or two out of the many in my heart of hearts. Then she motioned to have her hands *sponged* – some of the jelly annoying her: this was done, and she began to sleep again – the *last*, I saw. I felt she must be raised, took her in my arms, I felt the struggle to cough begin, and end unavailingly – no pain, no sigh, – only a quiet *sight*. Her head fell on me. I thought she might have fainted, but presently there was the least knitting of the brows, and A. cried 'Quest' anima benedetta è passata!'

It was so. She is with God, who takes from me the life of my life in one sense, – not so, in the truest. My life is fixed and sure now. I shall live out the remainder in her direct influence, endeavouring to complete mine, miserably imperfect now, but so as to take the good she was meant to give me. I go away from Italy at once, having no longer any business there: I have our child about whom I shall exclusively employ myself, doing her part by him. I shall live in the presence of her, in every sense, I hope and believe – so that so far my loss is not *irreparable* – but the future is nothing to me now, except inasmuch as it confirms and realizes the past. I cannot plan now, or at least talk about plans, but I shall leave Italy at once, only staying to take away the necessity of a return, for years at least. Pen has been perfect to me: he sate all yesterday with his arms round me; said things like her to me. I shall try and work hard, educate him, and live worthy of my past fifteen years' happiness. I do not feel paroxysms of grief, but as if the very blessing, she died giving me, insensible to all beside, had begun to work already. She will be buried tomorrow. Several times in writing this I have for a moment referred in my mind to her – 'I will ask Ba about that.' The grief of everybody is sincere, I am told. Everybody is kind in offers of help – all is done for me that can be; and it is not a little just now. Isa came at the early morning and stayed till night, taking away Pen. I shall now go in and sit with herself – my Ba, for ever. The service will be that of the Ch. of En., that I may hear those only words at the beginning. Bless you both, dearest papa and sis. I will write after tomorrow. Don't be in any concern for me, I have some of her strength, really, added to mine. Love to dear Milsand. Ever your own.

R. BROWNING

How she looks now – how perfectly beautiful!

EPILOGUE

At the midnight in the silence of the sleep-time,
    When you set your fancies free,
Will they pass to where – by death, fools think,
      imprisoned –
Low he lies who once so loved you, whom you loved so,
      – Pity me?

Oh to love so, be so loved, yet so mistaken!
    What had I on earth to do
With the slothful, with the mawkish, the unmanly?
Like the aimless, helpless, hopeless, did I drivel
      – Being – who?

One who never turned his back but marched breast
      forward,
    Never doubted clouds would break,
Never dreamed, though right were worsted, wrong
      would triumph,
Held we fall to rise, are baffled to fight better,
        Sleep to wake.

No, at noonday in the bustle of man's work-time
    Greet the unseen with a cheer!
Bid him forward, breast and back as either should be,
'Strive and thrive!' cry 'Speed, – fight on, fare ever
        There as here!'

ROBERT BROWNING

INDEX OF FIRST LINES

ELIZABETH BARRETT BROWNING

255